ARAMAIC LIGHT

ON GENESIS

Aramaic Old Testament Series
Volume 1

Books in print by Rocco A. Errico

Setting A Trap for God: The Aramaic Prayer of Jesus
Let There Be Light: The Seven Keys
And There Was Light
The Mysteries of Creation: The Genesis Story
The Message of Matthew: An Annotated Parallel Aramaic-English Gospel of Matthew
Classical Aramaic – Book 1

Spanish publication
La Antigua Oración Aramea de Jesús: El Padrenuestro

German publications
Das Aramaische Vaterunser
Es Werde Licht

Italian publication
Otto accordi con Dio: il Padre Nostro originario

Books in print by Rocco A. Errico and George M. Lamsa
Aramaic New Testament Series: Volumes 1 – 7
Aramaic Light on the Gospel of Matthew
Aramaic Light on the Gospels of Mark and Luke
Aramaic Light on the Gospel of John
Aramaic Light on the Acts of the Apostles
Aramaic Light on Romans through 2 Corinthians
Aramaic Light on Galatians through Hebrews
Aramaic Light on James through Revelation

Books in print by George M. Lamsa
The Holy Bible from the Ancient Eastern Text
Idioms in the Bible Explained & A Key to the Original Gospels
New Testament Origin
The Shepherd of All – The 23rd Psalm

ARAMAIC LIGHT
ON GENESIS

A commentary based on the Aramaic language
and ancient Near Eastern customs

Aramaic Old Testament Series
Volume 1

Rocco A. Errico / *George M. Lamsa*

The Noohra Foundation, Inc
Smyrna, Georgia

First Printing October 2007

ISBN: 978-0-9631292-2-2

To

Mrs. Donalyn Kling

with my deepest and most sincere appreciation for
your generous help and interest in the Aramaic work and
for making the publication of this commentary possible.

CONTENTS

Foreword by Rocco A. Errico xi

Introduction by Rocco A. Errico and George M. Lamsa xvii

Abbreviations xxxi

THE COMMENTARY

Introduction: *Aramaic Light on Genesis* 1

Chapter 1 5

Chapter 2 23

Chapter 3 42

Chapter 4 57

Chapter 5 66

Chapter 6 67

Chapter 7 72

Chapter 8 75

Chapter 9 78

Chapter 10 86

Chapter 11 91

Chapter 12 95

Chapter 13 99

Chapter 14 100

Chapter 15 106

Chapter 16 108

Chapter 17 111

Chapter 18 117

Chapter 19 122

Chapter 20 130

Chapter 21 133

Chapter 22 137

Chapter 23 141

Chapter 24 143

Chapter 25 148

Chapter 26 150

Chapter 27 152

Chapter 28 154

Chapter 29 156

Chapter 30 160

Chapter 31 162

Chapter 32 166

Chapter 33 169

Chapter 34 171

Chapter 35 174

Chapter 36 (no comments in this chapter)

Chapter 37 177

Chapter 38 179

Chapter 39 (no comments in this chapter)

Chapter 40 182

Chapter 41 183

Chapter 42 (no comments in this chapter)

Chapter 43 186

Chapter 44 190

Chapter 45 (no comments in this chapter)

Chapter 46 191

Chapter 47 195

Chapter 48 196

Chapter 49 198

Chapter 50 205

Bibliography. 207

About the Author—George M. Lamsa 213

About the Author—Rocco A. Errico 215

FOREWORD
By Rocco A. Errico

A Distinctive Commentary

Aramaic Light on Genesis is an unusual and incomparable commentary for many reasons. First, it provides a unique understanding of the ancient Semitic customs and culture. It illuminates difficult and puzzling passages of the Old Testament and offers unparalleled insight into the character and behavior of the people. This is possible because of the late Dr. George M. Lamsa, who was born in that part of the world where the very old, Semitic world's customs and manners were kept.

Dr. Lamsa, the originator and coauthor of this present commentary, was a native Aramaic speaking Assyrian who came from an area of the Near East where the people were still living and practicing much of their past cultural religious traditions. He grew up in that part of the age-old biblical land from which Abraham migrated to Palestine, known at that time as Canaan. His family lived a simple pastoral life, as did his ancestors during the time of the Hebrew patriarchs. Even to this day, these Aramaic speaking people converse in idioms and parables, some of which would be difficult for Westerners to comprehend. His people were direct descendants of the Assyrians, who also mixed with some of the dispersed northern ten tribes of Israel in the mountains of ancient Assyria. This area is known today as part of Iraq, and during Dr. Lamsa's time it was a part of Turkey.

Dr. W. A. Wigram, a noted English scholar, spent over ten years as a missionary and researcher in Kurdistan in that region of Turkey. Concerning the survival of the descendants of the ancient Assyrians and their cultural customs, Dr. Wigram writes:

A strange survival in an isolated corner of the world, these last representatives of the ancient Assyrian stock have hitherto kept up the most primitive of Semitic customs to an extent that can hardly be paralleled elsewhere, even in Mesopotamian marsh districts. As an ancient and fossilized Church, they had also preserved ecclesiastical rites and ceremonies which have either perished altogether elsewhere, or else have survived only in almost unrecognizable form. . . .Here are a people who, in the time of the beginning of the Christian era, are found living in the lands where, in the year 600 BC, the Assyrian stock had been established since history began; nor is there any record of any considerable immigration into, or emigration from, that land in the interval.

Their own traditions affirm that they are of the old Assyrian blood, with a possible intermixture of certain Babylonian or Chaldean elements. . . It was only natural that this old Semitic stock, living where nothing had ever occurred to disturb their habits of life, should keep up the old Semitic customs, **They still lived, or did live till the changes of the Great War brought about an alteration, the life of the Old Testament.** Bible customs or those that we call such, were, of course, not peculiar to the Hebrew, but were the common heritage of all the stock to which he belonged and a part of the atmosphere of the land.[1]

Dr. Lamsa's Original Commentary

When Dr. Lamsa wrote *Old Testament Light,* a commentary on Genesis to Malachi, 976 pages, his publisher and his friends advised him to comment only on the most difficult and important verses. They especially asked him to elucidate passages of Scripture that had become obscure through translation and misunderstanding of Near Eastern, Semitic word meanings, idioms, and culture. While he was preparing *Old Testament Light*, Dr. Lamsa was constantly aware of the size of the book. He did not want to create a very large volume that would burden the reader, nor did he wish to duplicate what one

---

[1]Dr. W. A. Wigram, *The Assyrians and Their Neighbors,* pp. 177-178, 185. The bold lettering was put by me for emphasis in this study of the Old Testament.

might find from other commentaries.

When *Old Testament Light* was published in 1964, it received much acclaim and publicity. This recognition brought requests from various regions in the United States and Canada for a more expanded exposition on many passages that he only lightly explained and for further enlightenment on others in which he made no comments. These requests were made during the time when Dr. Lamsa and I were collaborating between the years 1965 to 1972. So in the early 1970s we drafted additional material on the Old Testament, but these new works were not completed.

Now with the kind and generous permission of Dr. Lamsa's niece, Mrs. David (Nina) Shabaz and the entire Shabaz family, I have been editing, expanding, annotating and preparing Dr. Lamsa's previous volume in a new format. I am also adding more comments derived from my continual research in the Aramaic language and completing the comments that Dr. Lamsa and I had only drafted.

Formation of this Commentary

Dr. Lamsa and I had worked together for ten years before he passed from this earthly life on September 22, 1975. I have been lecturing, writing, teaching, and continuing the Aramaic approach to holy Scripture since his passing. Before Dr. Lamsa became ill, he told me how he wanted the new commentary on the Old Testament to be published in separate volumes to aid Bible students and minsters who were interested in this approach to the Bible.

Aramaic Light on Genesis is not a commentary founded on contemporary academic analysis of Scripture nor on modern interpretations. It does not use critical source/historical and literary methods of interpretation. Occasionally, however, in the footnotes I do make reference to some of the modern, scholarly material on the books of the Old Testament.

The reader must keep in mind that this commentary works with the received text—that is, with the Old Testament as we now have it in its present form—and does not attempt to provide the reader with source/critical studies. I use laymen's language and not theological, specialized terminology. As much as possible, each comment is written in story form. This style will be maintained throughout the *Aramaic Old Testament Series,* beginning with Genesis and continuing through Malachi.

The comments also contain quotes of scriptural passages from *The Holy Bible from the Ancient Eastern Text* by Dr. George M. Lamsa. These quotations are identified as the "Aramaic Peshitta text, Lamsa translation." There are other citations of Scripture in the body of the comments that I have translated directly from the Eastern Aramaic Peshitta text. These passages are identified as "Aramaic Peshitta text, Errico."

I have attempted as much as possible to avoid a collision with denominational interpretations and theological implications. However, in certain passages cited in this volume, it became unavoidable. Apparently some biblical interpreters have unwittingly formed and established monumental dogmas and confusing notions on verses that were only idioms, metaphors or cultural customs.

According to Scripture, God, through revelation, had told the prophets to write in a plain and simple language.[2] But, because of translating from one language to another, adding and omitting from Scripture, and a lack of translators, many passages of scripture have suffered losses. Thousands of these verses that were once clear in their original state became obscure and the subject of theological controversies. Both the literalist interpreter and the modern thinker have contributed to a misunderstanding of Scripture, not through a fault of their own, but because the Bible comes to us from a culture distinct from our forms of thinking and reasoning.

---

[2]See Dt. 27:8 and Hab. 2:2.

Acknowledgments and Final Word

My deep appreciation and sincere gratitude to the entire Shabaz family as proprietors of the Lamsa estate for their kind and most gracious permission to edit, revise, expand, annotate, and prepare Dr. Lamsa's previous commentary *Old Testament Light* in this new format.

My very genuine and heartfelt thanks and gratefulness to Ms. Sue Edwards, Mrs. Ann Milbourn, Ms. Linetta Izenman and Mr. Hanny Freiwat for their constructive suggestions and assistance in preparing this manuscript for publication. In addition, the board of the Noohra Foundation and I are extremely thankful to Mrs. Donalyn Kling, whose generosity and dedication to the Aramaic work made this publication possible.

To all readers of this commentary I say: *Tybootha washlama dalaha nehwoon amhon hasha walmeen!* "The grace (lovingkindness) and peace of God are with you now and always!"

Rocco A. Errico
September 2007

INTRODUCTION

An Aramaic Approach

Throughout the centuries there have been many commentaries written on the greatest of all books, the Bible. Scholars of all races and from various countries have, one way or another, attempted to bring a clearer understanding of Holy Scripture. And yet, even to this day, people of all ages are more eager than ever to comprehend the book that contains life, light, and truth.

This commentary is based on the Aramaic language and ancient biblical culture, customs, and manners that played an important role in recording the Bible. Interestingly, the Aramaic word for commentary is *nohara*, "to throw light" or "to enlighten."

In the very ancient days, because of the fact that words and phrases had several meanings, all important state or royal decrees, treaties, and agreements contained marginal explanations or commentaries so that there would be no doubt left in the mind of the reader as to their exact meaning. "And in the days of Artakhshisht, wrote Bishlam, Mahderat, Tabaiel, and the rest of their companions to Artakhshisht king of Persia; and the letter was written in Aramaic and interpreted in Aramaic."[1]

The purpose of this *nohara* is to present a Semitic, Near Eastern understanding of scriptural passages that have been somewhat obscured through translations and to bring to light words that have been unwittingly mistranslated and recover their lost meanings. Its further aim is to explain biblical idioms, metaphors, allegories, visions, dreams, customs, and manners that in their ancient context are difficult and unfamiliar to Western minds but simple for Near Easterners to understand. After all, what we refer to as the "Old Testament" (Genesis to Malachi) was written first in Semitic

---

[1] Ezra 4:7, Eastern Aramaic Peshitta text, Lamsa translation.

languages. It was written for Semitic people, centuries before Greek, Latin, and present European languages were born. Also, what we call the "New Testament" was written for the descendants of the same people. So many of the authors of this sacred literature were inspired by God's Spirit. They lived in a world of unseen, invisible realities.

The Style of Commentary

This is not a verse-by-verse commentary. We have commented only on those passages that needed greater clarification. This is a book for ministers, Bible students, and lay-people who are eager to understand the meaning of Scripture and ancient customs and manners that constitute the biblical background.

In truth, what often appears as hard, harsh, ambiguous, challenging, and difficult in Scripture was easily understood by the people to whom the Bible was written. It is still well understood by the descendants of the races and people who, centuries ago, played a dominant part in one of the world's greatest sacred dramas, the history of the Bible. The reason for this is that in biblical lands most of the ancient culture, customs, idioms, figurative speech, psychology, and mannerisms had remained unchanged until the dawn of the early 1900s.

The way of life and thinking of the people who lived at the time when biblical scribes penned this sacred literature were handed down in their context in our century as though they were embedded in amber. The truth that the Bible contains was to be revealed and written in Semitic languages and preserved in its purity for the generations to come. There was always a remnant of people that kept the spiritual light burning amidst darkness, persecution, and suffering. Spiritual truth endures forever.

The Term Bible

Our English term "Bible" comes from the old French *Bible*. The French word derives from the Latin and Greek, *Biblia*. The term itself derives from the name of a small town in Syria called *Biblos*, where papyrus was manufactured. It means "books" or a "library." In English, we are accustomed to calling the Jewish and Christian Scriptures the Holy Bible. In ancient times, however, people did not ordinarily refer to the sacred book as the Holy Bible. According to the Jewish writers Philo and Josephus, the usual term was the "Writings" or "Scriptures."

The Bible as a "library" contains inspired writings of the Hebrew prophets and also the recordings of the temple and court scribes. Scripture is an important surviving library from the past, containing sacred teachings originally written in a plain alphabet that people could read and understand. It also contains many volumes that deal with various phases of life, such as law, drama, history, poetry, philosophy, art, science, religion and forms of worship. Many episodes are recordings of revelation coming from an invisible world but written in the language of this world.

Its Semitic Meaning

In the Semitic languages of Aramaic and Hebrew, the term Bible does not mean a "library." The Old Testament in Hebrew is designated as the *Tanakh,* an acronym referring to the *Torah* (the first five books of Moses: Genesis through Deuteronomy), *Nevim* (The Prophets), and *Kituvim* (The Writings). Although most scholars translate the Semitic word *Torah* as the "law," it has a much deeper meaning, such as "teaching, enlightenment."

In Aramaic, the language of the Hebrew patriarchs, it is called *Auretha* (pronounced *oraytha*). According to Aramaic and Hebrew, both *Torah* and *Auretha* derive from the Semitic root *Yhr* and mean, "to direct, teach, instruct" and, by inference, "to enlighten."

Dr. Lamsa also suggests that the term *auretha* derives from the Aramaic root *ra*, which means "to see through the mind." The adjective of this verb in Aramaic is *reyana*. Spiritual truths cannot be seen by the human eye or easily explained in words. They are conceived and understood through the mind and a higher intelligence. No other name could have been more suitable for a book that contains spiritual laws, ordinances, and moral ethics. As the psalmist aptly puts it: "Thy word is a lamp to my feet and a light to my path."[2]

Spiritual Concepts

Alaha, the Aramaic word for God, is the essence of life. *Alaha* can neither be seen with the physical eyes nor understood in human descriptions and concepts alone; but we can comprehend God as a loving, caring parent, and we can sense the divine presence. What is spiritual and infinite cannot be seen or described in the language of mortal and finite beings. Also, God as creator and eternal Spirit, is the Holistic environment of the entire universe and cannot be fully portrayed, divided, nor defined by its creations. On the other hand, where a spiritual idea cannot be pictured or described in words, it can be imparted in a parable, allegory, and in figurative speech. This is the reason some of the prophets portrayed God as an emperor, unapproachable, surrounded by ministers, counselors, and intermediaries. Some of the biblical writers also presented God with hands, feet, ears, and eyes. They described God as sometimes happy, sometimes sorry, and sometimes furious and extremely wrathful.

The reader needs to realize that the Israelites were forbidden to draw pictures, carve statues, or make graven images of God. They could not make objects of worship. But the Hebrew prophets found another way to portray and explain spiritual ideas and matters so that

---

[2]Ps. 119:105, Eastern Aramaic Peshitta text, Lamsa translation.

even common folk could understand them. They used parables and allegories that the people could easily grasp but never took literally. These prophets were skilled in the use of their language and were familiar with the common idiomatic expressions and hyperboles. For example, when women singers said that Saul had slain his thousands and David his tens of thousands, the people knew that what they meant was that David had slain Goliath and had become a greater warrior than Saul. They knew that it was a poetic song composed by dancing women that acknowledged David's bravery and strength. The general public knew it was a song of triumph to glorify God.

God is the spiritual essence of life and intelligence that governs the entire universe. A physical God is man's own idea and invention. God is truth, life, and light; therefore, God must be understood spiritually. Furthermore, according to the Hebrew story of creation, everything that God created was perfect and good; hence God is not the author of evil, nor is evil a reality.

Readers of Scripture need to realize that there is a human element in the Bible just as there is usually a certain amount of copper or brass in gold. And it is this human ingredient that pictures God—the source of love—as angry, sorry, and repenting of the wrong that was done. On the other hand, in the second chapter of Genesis, the spiritual and immortal being is reduced to a physical and mortal man so that the author could relate the story of humankind's departure from its inner, spiritual nature and moral law. How can one portray a spirit eating forbidden fruit, finding itself naked and being ashamed, then clothed in fig leaves or in skins. In other words, the second narrative of creation is written to reveal how and why humanity lost a consciousness of abundant and graceful living.

The Bible is an ancient and authentic written record where one can read of God's dealing with men and women and the divine interest in humanity. According to Jesus' teaching, God is like a father who is interested in his children. Nearly all great religions have some kind of deity—a revelation from, or mystic communication with, a higher power. However, the sacred book of the Hebrews teaches a monotheistic approach to God, which is the underlying root and interconnectedness of all humankind, a spiritual and clear concept of God, and an understanding of divine love and direct communications with humanity.

The Influence of the Bible

About four thousand years ago, God appeared to Abraham in a vision and told him that by his seed (teaching) all of the nations would be blessed. Two thousand years later, Jesus of Nazareth, a devout country Jew, read the holy books that contained these divine promises, studied them, and then began to open the way and demonstrate how to bring them into fulfillment. Because of this, he became a great light to enlighten the world. Despite many world changes, wars, persecutions, and the rise and fall of many great empires, God's promises never failed, nor were they forgotten by the Jews, who had shed rivers of blood for them.

Today, the whole world, one way or another, is leavened with the moral ethics and truths that centuries ago were revealed to the Hebrew patriarchs and prophets. The Jewish moral and spiritual ethics as taught by Jesus of Nazareth have become the ethics of many countries. No false promises or testaments could have survived all these centuries, and nothing could have enriched and consoled the hearts of humankind, more than the simple teaching of Scripture.

The Bible, therefore, is a witness to God's revelations and inspiration for the benefit of humanity. One may refer to this sacred book as a guide to lead humanity to God—that is, to peace, harmony, health, and prosperity. One must also realize that the book was written by men who had some experience with God and who had heard the divine inner voice. It is a book of guidance in all phases of human relations; throughout the centuries, humanity has never been able to dispense with it, and nothing has been able to replace it as a book for edification and consolation.

Bible Based on Dreams and Visions

The great literature was revealed in dreams and visions in arid deserts, caves, and on the tops of mountains. And the simple pious people, like the prophets, believed in their dreams, visions, and divine communications. The Israelites were directed and guided in all their wandering in the desert by a great spiritual power that they could not see or touch. This is why a large portion of Scripture is based on visions and revelations. Many of these truths were revealed in symbols and metaphors so that the people might understand them and remember them.

It is not easy to describe ideas such as depression, famine, suffering, joy, or sadness. But they can be revealed in symbols through one's dreams and visions. For example, the author of Genesis records that Pharaoh saw fat cows and lean cows and full ears of wheat and blasted ears of wheat, indicating through symbols times of plenty and times of famine. Joseph, being a student of spiritual matters and interpreter of visions and dreams, knew the meaning of the symbols in Pharaoh's dream.

It is important for students of the Bible to know something about inner-voice visions and dreams and their meaning, especially for Bible interpretation. For instance, it was in a dream that Jacob wrestled with an angel.[3] The angel bore the face of Esau. After his vision, the next day Jacob said to Esau: " . . . because now I have seen your face, as I saw the face of an angel, and you were pleased with me."[4] In Aramaic, pious men are often called angels. But real angels are spirits; they have no bodies with which to wrestle someone. Jacob wrestled in his disturbed mind and heart. He had deceived his brother Esau and, therefore, he had a guilty conscience.[5]

It was in a vision that Abraham entertained God and his two emissaries (angels) and served them food of which they partook. Also

---

[3]Gen. 32:24-29.
[4]Gen. 33:10, Lamsa translation.
[5]Gen. 32:11.

in a vision, the prophet Isaiah saw angels worshiping God, and in a vision Ezekiel traveled in spirit to Jerusalem and measured the temple. According to the author of the book of Daniel, through the medium of visions and dreams, Daniel saw the rise and fall of many empires.

In biblical days, kings, princes, and the people depended on the prophets and God's revelations for guidance, healing, prosperity, and protection. Moreover, prophets and men of God acted as statesmen and counselors to kings and princes. Both the people and their leaders were looking to God for help, guidance, and the fulfillment of the divine promises.

Indeed, in those ancient days, writing was in its infancy and learned men were few. Therefore, the prophets wrote in a simple, pictorial, and clear style, free from ifs, buts, and other qualifying clauses that often obscured truth. They wrote in a plain manner, using short sentences so that the simple and unlearned folk might understand their messages, heed their admonitions, and turn from the wrong paths. These courageous men of God did not hide anything from their people; neither were they afraid of kings and princes, who were often opposed to God's way, truth, and reforms for the nation of Israel.

Biblical authors were not interested in literary style or in degrees. Their main objective was to impart the revealed truths to the ears and eyes of a people who thought and spoke in simple speech and who counted numbers on their fingers. And yet the beauty and the style of Scripture has never been surpassed. Its simplicity has produced an inspiring and lasting literature.

Ancient Customs, Idioms, and Mannerisms

Nevertheless, the Bible contains many expressions and mannerisms of speech, local idioms that no foreigner without the ancient Semitic language, background, and issues could understand.

For example, three thousand years ago, the psalmist wrote: "They that sow in tears shall reap in joy. He who goes forth and weeps, bearing precious seed, shall doubtless come again with rejoicing, bringing his sheaves with him."[6] The people who heard these words certainly understood what the psalmist meant. In Palestine every family in one way or another felt the scarcity of bread during the sowing season, when the family food supplies that had been stored in the fall were exhausted, and the children at home were crying for bread. Even in certain areas of the Near East in modern times, certain farmers weep as they scatter the precious seed in the ground, while their children at home are famished. But during the harvest season, the tears change to joy, and on the first day of the harvest, people celebrate because bread is abundant and the children would soon be filled and happy.

Many ministers and Bible students in the West would hardly know why the sower wept as he scattered seed. European and American farmers simply sow and plant and are seldom short of bread. In the West, countries work to build a surplus of wheat and other food supplies. In the same way, of course, American customs and ways of life are difficult for a foreigner to comprehend.

From Genesis to Malachi, biblical writers employed many idiomatic expressions. Here are various examples: "The suckling child shall play on the hole of the asp"[7] means that a small nation will not be afraid of a powerful nation. "The weaned child shall put his hand on the cockatrice den"[8] means a small nation will be able to handle or negotiate with their deadly enemies. "The lion shall eat straw like an ox"[9]— powerful nations will be satisfied with what they have and not seek to devour small nations.

Further examples: "My spirit shall not dwell in man forever"[10]

---

[6]Ps. 126:5-6, K. J. V.

[7]Isa. 11:8, K. J. V.

[8]Isa. 11:8, K. J. V.

[9]Isa. 11:7, K. J. V.

[10]Gen. 6:3, Lamsa translation.

—I have become weary and impatient. "She became a pillar of salt"[11]—she suffered a stroke and became lifeless, stricken dead. "I have lifted up my hands"[12]—I have taken a solemn oath. "He hath sold us"[13]—He has devoured our dowry. There are over a thousand idioms throughout the Bible that were translated exactly, but their meaning was misunderstood.

It is only natural that such idioms should be misunderstood and misinterpreted. And just as the Aramaic idioms and metaphors are difficult and challenging for Western people, so English, French, and German idioms are hard for Near Easterners to understand. For example, no Near Eastern Semite would understand such phrases as: "he lost his shirt," "He died on third base," "He was born with a silver spoon in his mouth," "She has been living in hot water for six months," "She and her friend were chewing the rag when I arrived," "I am in a jam." Many other such sayings bewilder foreign students.

On the other hand, idioms, metaphors, parables, and poetic phrases, when translated from one language into another, often lose their original meaning. It is difficult to find equivalent words to give the same shade of meaning. And parables that derive from the customs of the people sometimes have no comparison in other countries. Therefore, in reading the English versions of the Bible, we need to keep in mind that we are reading a translation of a translation of a translation of the Scriptures into a totally alien and modern tongue—a language that did not even exist when the Bible was written.

Therefore, a reader may be bewildered when reading contradictory and seemingly repulsive sayings in Scripture. For example, Genesis 6:6 reads: "And it repented the Lord that he had made man . . . and it grieved him at his heart."[14] And yet another passage reads:

---

[11]Gen. 19:26, K. J. V.

[12]Gen. 14:22, Lamsa translation.

[13]Gen. 31:15, K. J. V.

[14]There are a few other passages of scripture where the Lord repents: Gen 6:7 and 1 Sam. 15:11.

". . . for he [The Lord] is not a man that he should repent."[15]

Many idioms and figures of speech are still in use in biblical lands. But in Western languages, words change and, like cars, become obsolete. Near Eastern people still say, "He flew over the river," meaning, "he crossed the river." All languages have similar problems. For example, many English words have several meanings, such as "fresh, light, and lead." The meaning of such words is always determined by the context.

For years, missionaries have been confronted by many difficulties in converting Muslims, Jews, and many other races in the Near East to Christianity. They don't realize that among the greatest obstacles in the way of these people are the mistranslations and contradictions in various Bible versions. Even hundreds of Near Eastern Christians, Assyrians, Arabs, and Armenians, were horrified when they read in different translations that were given to them that one must hate his father, mother, wife, brother, his children, and his own life in order to be a follower of Jesus of Nazareth. Hundreds of Bibles were burned because of such mistranslations. Translators did not know that what Jesus really said was that unless you *put aside* or *set aside* your father and mother and so forth you could not be his disciple.

We must always keep in mind that both the Old and New Testaments were written by different prophets, scribes, and disciples at different periods of history. The five books of Moses were written about a thousand years before the book of Malachi, the last book in the Old Testament. When Moses wrote, he and the Hebrews were wandering in a harsh and waste desert, while Malachi was living and writing under the rule of the mighty and well-organized Persian Empire. The Persians had championed the cause of the Jews. At that time, the world had advanced in its culture and institutions.

Therefore, readers of Scripture need to realize something about the geographical conditions, political situations, and the influences of the period in which any given portion of scripture was written. There

---

[15]1 Sam. 15:29, K. J. V. See also Num. 23:19.

were many current issues that both the writer and his original readers and listeners understood. There was no need to explain such issues and the underlying causes that had created them.

Our Times

Today we are living in a mechanized and technological world. The wooden threshing instrument is forever gone; cars, trucks, and planes have replaced donkeys, mules, camels, carts, and oxen. In our world, because of our scientific knowledge and our abundant supply of wheat, no farmer ties the mouths of his oxen; no one ever sees a donkey's mill or a threshing sledge. Women no longer sit behind the stone, grinding their meal. And no virgins carry lamps to greet the bridegroom and bride. The day in which wine, milk, and butter were stored in sheepskins is gone; the skins are replaced by glass containers that never burst. The whole way of life has changed from biblical days. And the change has left a chasm of about 3,500 years between us and the time when some portions of the Bible were written.

This commentary is an attempt to bridge that chasm. It opens hundreds of passages, some of which have lost their meaning through mistranslation, some because idioms were translated literally, and others because of the lack of knowledge of the background, customs, manners, metaphors, issues, and allegories that existed during the time of the writer. Still other misinterpretations are due to the lack of knowledge of the Semitic languages and the subtle use of certain words and allegorical ways through which the spiritual truth and understanding were interwoven and imparted.

The primary objective in this work, as it was in the seven-volume Aramaic New Testament commentary series (Matthew through Revelation), is to take the reader to biblical lands and to see and understand the Bible through the eyes of the Near East.

As much as possible we have attempted to avoid doctrinal and theological matters. This work is based on the Near Eastern, Semitic understanding of Scripture, the Aramaic culture from which it sprang, and the Semitic languages in which it was written by the holy prophets and scribes. These men were inspired by the Spirit of God to record their spiritual truths, admonitions, and lessons.

An Important Note: The Term "Semitic"

Unless otherwise indicated, when the term "Semitic" and "Semite" are used in this commentary, they refer to the behavior and beliefs that apply both to Near Eastern Jews who kept the customs and manners of the ancient Middle East as well as to all other Semitic peoples, such as Assyrians, Syrians (Arameans), Chaldeans, Arabs and other Semitic races. (These terms do not apply to Western Semitic peoples.) The original spelling of "Semitic" was "Shemitic," which derives from Shem, one of the sons of Noah.

Concluding Remarks

It is our sincere belief that once we know and understand truth, that very truth will set us free from doubt, contradictions, controversies, and strife. It will untie us from misunderstanding and free us for a common cause that will hasten God's reign—that is, the reign of peace, justice, and harmony for which the Hebrew prophets, Jesus of Nazareth, and his apostles gave their lives.

Only by recognizing that all humanity is one family can we save ourselves and refrain from destroying our world with the instruments of annihilation that we have devised with our own hands. It will take spiritual light, truth, and love with the desire to practice and demonstrate them in our lives that will usher in a new age for our world.

Holy Scripture offers a way out of our dilemma through the simple and all encompassing truths it teaches. But this way has to be carefully and correctly gleaned from the various books of the Bible.

All humanity is of one origin and one source and we must realize this in practical ways so that we as human beings may continue our evolution in higher consciousness that will lead us toward greater understanding and harmony.

I am grateful to the hundreds of men and women who have enabled me to continue the Aramaic work that Dr. Lamsa began in the early 1930s. Dr. Lamsa was especially thankful for the years of faithful contributors who helped him when he was translating the Bible from Aramaic into English and when writing commentaries and other books on the Bible. He also sincerely and deeply appreciated the United States of America with its free institutions and cultural freedom of expression.

Rocco A. Errico and George M. Lamsa

ABBREVIATIONS

Hebrew Bible (Old Testament)

Gen.	Genesis	Prov.	Proverbs
Ex.	Exodus	Eccl.	Ecclesiastes
Lev.	Leviticus	Sol.	Song of Solomon
Num.	Numbers	Isa.	Isaiah
Dt.	Deuteronomy	Jer.	Jeremiah
Jos.	Joshua	Ezk.	Ezekiel
Sam.	Samuel	Dan	Daniel
Ki.	Kings	Obad.	Obadiah
Chron.	Chronicles	Hab.	Habakkuk
Ps.	Psalms	Zech.	Zechariah

New Testament

Mt.	Matthew
Mk.	Mark
Lk.	Luke
Jn.	John
Rom.	Romans
Heb.	Hebrews
Rev.	Revelation

Other Abbreviations

BCE Before the Common Era (BC)

CE   Common Era (AD)

K.J.V. King James Version

ܡܩܒܐ ܕܒܝܬ ܓܙܐ

INTRODUCTION TO GENESIS

Genesis is the first book of the *Pentateuch.* The term *Pentateuch* is a Greek translation of the Aramaic or biblical term *Hamsha Sepreh di Mosheh,* "The five books of Moses," which are Genesis, Exodus, Leviticus, Numbers, and Deuteronomy. Jewish authorities refer to these books as the *Torah.* The Hebrew title of the first book in the Bible is not Genesis but *B'reshith,* meaning "In the Beginning." In those ancient days, it was a common practice for scribes to title a book with its opening word or words. In Aramaic, however, Genesis is titled *Brita (pronounced Breeta),* "Creation." Genesis is a Greek title meaning "Origin."

Although the primary objective of Genesis is to present to the people of Israel the history of their ancestors and the origins of their faith, it also includes an account of the creation of heaven and earth and the origins of other peoples and nations. This background of the creation of the world and other races served as an introduction for the genealogies of the Hebrew patriarchs and of Abraham, acknowledged to be the father of the Hebrew faith. It presents a picture of their ancestral and cultural setting, language, and religion. The book traces Abraham's ancestry back to Adam and the divine declaration of hostility that would exist between humanity and the serpent.[1] The first eleven chapters are also written with all humankind in mind and not just the history of Israel and its faith.

The narratives and ideas in the book of Genesis were handed down orally and, according to Dr. Lamsa, it was written during the time of Moses.[2] It is believed that the entire work was guided by

---

[1]Gen. 3:15.

[2]Modern scholars believe that Genesis was written much later with many different authors known as J, E, P, and R. For further explanation of this German theory see Errico, Rocco A., *Mysteries of Creation:* The Genesis Story, "Authorship" pp. 10-11. Since this commentary is not based on contemporary academic analysis of Scripture, it does not employ critical source/historical and

1

divine inspiration. Its purpose was not to explain God's creations from a scientific point of view but to offer the idea that the Lord God of Israel was the Creator of the heavens and the earth and that other so-called gods did not create the cosmic system but were gods created by human beings.

There are two accounts of the creation story recorded in Genesis. The first, Genesis 1:1-31 and 2:1-3, is the spiritual account. God acts as a powerful deity, creating everything by command. The second record is an explanation or a commentary on the first creation story. Verse 4 of chapter 2 is a transitory scriptural passage that leads into the second account of creation.

It is most likely that for many centuries the two creation stories and other sacred creation material circulated by word of mouth and also may have been written on separate scrolls or tablets. Only after many years were these accounts edited and combined into a single work. Some of these accounts were written by different scribes. Marginal notes were often incorporated into the text and copied by later scribes.

Genesis contains some of these scribal notations, as do many other books of the Bible. For example: "The prayers of David the son of Jesse are ended."[3] This note was written to facilitate the reader's understanding of the book. Two quotes in Isaiah—"The burden of Babylon, which Isaiah the son of Amos did see"[4] and "The burden of Damascus"[5]—are further examples of marginal comments that were made a part of the text.

Genesis narrates a story that begins with the creation of the world and ends with the death of Joseph in Egypt. The first eleven chapters deal with universal aspects of the human condition, and the remaining 38 chapters deal with the lives of Abraham, Isaac, Jacob and his

---

literary methods of interpretation. Occasionally, there are references in the footnotes to some of the modern, scholarly material.

[3]Ps. 72:20, K. J. V.
[4]Isa. 13:1, K. J. V.
[5]Isa. 17:1, K. J. V.

twelve sons. It is also probable that the first eleven chapters derive from separate Near Eastern traditions that were edited and incorporated as an introduction to the narratives of the Hebrew patriarchs.

According to Jewish biblical scholars, the major theme of the book is God's role in human affairs. God created the world and made human beings to work in it and care for it. But humanity kept continually turning away from God; therefore, according to the narrator, God called Abraham to begin anew for humanity and to be the father of a particular people who would fulfill the divine will and reveal it to other peoples. All the families of the earth were to be blessed through Abraham's descendants, their faithfulness to God, and their practice of God's guidance. Some of the other themes are: The unity of the entire human family; its proclivity for good or evil; human rebellion; and the covenants between God, Abraham, and his descendants.

CHAPTER 1

Timeless Universe

In the beginning God created the heaven and the earth. Gen. 1:1.

The Aramaic text reads: "God created the heavens and the earth in the very beginning."[1] God is the subject of the sentence, and the heavens and the earth are the direct objects of the verb "created." The author informs us that the heavens and the earth were created from the very beginning—that is, before the present cosmic system as we now know it came into existence. In other words, the substance of heaven and earth were always in existence before the measuring of time.

Literally, the first verse reads: *Brasheeth bra alaha yath shmaya wyath araa,* "God created the essence heaven and the essence earth in the very beginning." The Aramaic word *yath* means "being, substance, existence, essence." In Hebrew, however, the word is *eth,* which is an untranslatable grammatical term that refers to the direct objects of the verb, the heavens and the earth.

In time and through greater insight and comprehension, humanity will come to know and understand many mysteries of the universe. Nonetheless, the author's emphasis is that there is only one premise and one power behind all manifestations of creation; he calls that one power and principle "God" (*Elohim* in Hebrew, *Alaha* in Aramaic). In the ancient Near Eastern world, most people believed that creation came into existence through a creator-deity or deities. They would not question the sovereignty and creative powers of the gods. The key to clearly understanding this ancient writing is to realize that this creation epic is a Semitic, Near Eastern prose poem, a literary depiction and not a literal description of creation.

---

[1]Gen. 1:1, Eastern Aramaic Peshitta text, Lamsa translation.

THE PHRASE "IN THE BEGINNING"

There was no beginning. What the opening passage of Scripture implies is that the reckoning of time was non-existent in the very beginning. To assume that God had just begun creating would be to limit God's omniscience. The universe is timeless and was always in existence though not in its present shape or form. There is no such thing as non-existence. (It is a difficult challenge for the human mind to comprehend a non-existent state. It is only because death appears to physical sight as annihilating existence that the mind creates the notion of non-existence. The process of death only annihilates the present physical form.) God, humanity, and the universe are from everlasting to everlasting. According to Scripture, the heavens declare the glory of God, and without its existence God would be robbed of glory.

The universe has undergone many changes and processes, but its essence and existence are eternal. Matter is energy and energy is light. Light is the essence of everything in the universe.[2] Form changes but the essence is the same. For example, in the beginning the earth may not have been as it appears to us now, but its substance is eternal regardless of its shape or appearance.

Scientists claim that the planet earth is four and a half billion years old, but this is hypothetical. On the other hand, four and a half billion years would be considered eternity. It is presumptuous to set a date to the existence of the universe and God's involvement with creation.

THE TERM "GOD"

It is extremely difficult to define God. Our English term "God" comes from Teutonic roots and has been associated by St. Boniface with the German word *gut,* meaning "good."[3] Its usage began about

---

[2]See Gen. 1:3.

[3]St. Boniface (680–754 CE) was known as the "Apostle of Germany."

6

the 14th century CE. and was known only among Teutonic peoples. God was known as the source of all life because it is God who constantly pours out life.

We can gain some insight about what the term "God" meant to the biblical writers by defining its Semitic root meaning. The root of both the Aramaic and Hebrew terms for God—*Alaha, Elohim*—is assumed to be derived from *Elh.* אלה. There are several mainline theories about the meaning of this root in Semitic languages: (1) The strong or mighty one, (2) the revered one, (3) the highest one, (4) helper, supporter, one who sustains.

Another Aramaic term for God is *Ithea,* "self-existent," "self-cohesive and sustaining." This term is qualitative and refers to the eternal existence, i.e., something that exists of itself and does not derive its life from anywhere or through anything else.

In those ancient days, God was also called the Most High God. This was done so that the people would distinguish the God of the Hebrews from other deities. God is truly nameless but is known by various names to all races and peoples; in Scripture itself, God has been given many different names. The major biblical Hebrew name that God is known by is *YHWH,* which has been translated as LORD, *Adonai*, and in Aramaic, *Mariah.*

Among the Semitic peoples of the Near East, no attempt was made to comprehend or define the mystery of God, nor did they question the existence of God. The closest meaning Westerners might understand concerning the Godhead is that it is the foundational, principle presence, substance, or premise upon which the entire universe and humanity subsists.[4] A Jewish writer and scholar, Robert Gordis, states: "It is true that the ancient Hebrews, unlike the Greeks, evinced no outstanding talent for scientific thought. Yet, incredibly, it was Genesis rather than the Greek philosophers and scientists that arrived at the concept of a 'uni-verse' created by one will and hence

---

[4]For a more detailed study and insight into the first chapter of Genesis, the meaning of God, and the names of God, see Errico, Rocco A., *The Mysteries of Creation: The Genesis Story.*

governed by universal laws of nature."

THE TERM "CREATED"

"Created" in Aramaic is *bra* and in Hebrew *bara*. It is an ancient Semitic term that the writer of the first verse presents as a special sense of creation by God and by this divine power alone. It does not infer creation out of nothing. It is only God who has created the awesome universe. By recognizing God as creator, humans are to respect the sacredness of the heavens and the earth. Poetically and metaphorically, God constructed the earth and its present form as a sacred sanctuary and the heavens as its ceiling or dome. God's action and presence permeate this glorious living temple.

Essence Without a Specific Form

And the earth was without form, and void; and darkness was upon the face of the deep. And the Spirit of God moved upon the face of the waters. Gen. 1:2.

The Aramaic text reads: "Now the earth was chaos and darkness was upon the deep [Oceans]. And the Spirit of God hovered compassionately over the surface of the waters."[5]

The two Semitic words that describe the idea that the earth was chaos are *toh* and *woh*. These two words mean to be empty of a specified form as we know form but not lacking essence. Its essence is spiritual, eternal, and indestructible, but the form is changeable, temporal, and destructible and depends on the substance that governs it.

At this time, the earth was not suitable for vegetation or any other forms of life. Earth was there but not in its present viable state,

---

[5]Gen. 1:2, Eastern Aramaic Peshitta text, Errico. For the complete translation, see Errico, Rocco A., *The Mysteries of Creation, The Genesis Story*, Chapter 2, pp. 20-31, in Aramaic and English.

hence the use of the word "chaos," in other words, "desolate, a wasteland." The second verse literally reads: "And the earth was [came to be] empty and desolate." In other words, it was nothing but confusion and chaos. But the essence, or creative force, was there.

Some biblical interpreters suggest that the earth may have suffered some catastrophic disruptions as the result of inner stresses, such as volcanic eruptions and earthquakes. The surface of the moon reveals such marks of volcanic disturbances. However that may have been, the earth was seemingly void of the forces and equilibrium that make order and life possible.

Nonetheless, the chaotic and uninhabitable matter may have been in existence ages before order and life appeared on the earth. The creation of the firmament, the sun, the moon, and the stars made order, time, and life possible. We may conclude that at the outset the earth was not capable of producing life and lacked precision, balance, and harmony.

THE DEEP, DARKNESS, AND GOD'S SPIRIT

Unrelenting chaos, incessant darkness, and unbounded waters were the evils, fears, and horrors of the ancient Near East. This verse depicts a stark and foreboding picture of all these elements at the beginning of God's creative works. The author makes a startling contrast between these feared forces and God's creative presence. Everything is excessively dark. The essence or substance of earth is in a non-differentiated state. The "deep" is the ocean. The creator's dynamic spirit symbolizes motion—the basic element for change. It also symbolizes the opposite principle of desolation embodied in the darkness and the deep.

"Hovered" is a translation of the Hebrew *mrahpeth* and the Aramaic *mraphah*. The Semitic root *mrp* means "to flutter, to shake." This form of the verb does not have the sense of brooding. It implies motion, a gentle movement. The word also means "to hover tremulously." In Aramaic, however, *mrahpah* in its root also means "to pity, cherish, to have compassion."

9

The author does not reveal anything about the origin of darkness, nor does he make known that God explicitly created it. Nevertheless, verse one implies that God created darkness because *Alaha* or *Elohim* created everything. Isaiah, the great Hebrew prophet, clearly attributes the existence of darkness to divine creation: "I form light and create darkness; I make peace and create hardships; I, the Lord, do all these things."[6]

Light

And God said, Let there be light: and there was light. Gen. 1:3.

The term "light" refers to a brightness or a shining. There had to be light first in order to bring a distinction between the light and the darkness (see verse 4). Science teaches that matter is nothing more than gravitationally trapped light or energy. *Noohra*, in Aramaic, means "light, sight, insight, brightness, brilliance, enlightenment, understanding." Light is the essence of all substance. Everything in the universe is reducible to light. All matter, before manifesting in particular forms such as trees, plants, etc., is pure light. Present in all form is a hidden pattern. The pattern or essence is its own light, which will eventually come forth in its distinctive shape.

But the notion of light coming first is a biblical idea. Light was necessary so that the creative work could be divided into time. In other words, temporal creation preceded spatial work:

The first three acts of creation are not as it were the manufacture of substances, but the basic divisions of the universe. Separation of light from darkness is temporal, not spatial. The creation of light is put before these divisions because it renders possible the temporal succession into which the world is set. . .God creates brightness and thereby makes possible the basic cycle of time

---

[6]Isa. 45:7, Eastern Aramaic Peshitta text, Lamsa translation.

and order.[7]

Metaphorically, "light" means "enlightenment; that is, light represents the knowledge of God and the moral law. Light is also symbolic of life, joy, justice, and deliverance. Holy Scripture states that light clothes God: "You cover yourself with light like a mantle."[8]

For many centuries humankind felt the presence of God or a great governing force, but humanity knew little or nothing about God's presence, the natural forces that surrounded all life, nor did they know much about the moral law.

The author tells us that the sun was created on the fourth day, and, yet, there were evening and morning on the previous days. This is poetic speech describing a unit of time such as "first day" or "second day," a period based on the seven known planets. The sun was created on the fourth day after the trees and grass were created. Again, we must keep in mind this is a literary depiction of creation, not a literal description, that forms a poetic pattern. Day one corresponds with day four, day two with day five and day three with day six. This is referred to in Aramaic/Hebrew poetry as parallelism.[9] Interestingly, pristine societies unpretentiously reasoned and observed that brightness (light) always came before the appearance of the sun; therefore, the light (brightness) acted as a herald of its coming source.

The First Day

And God called the light Day, and the darkness he called Night. And the evening and the morning were the first day. Gen. 1:5.

Before the term "day" was used, human knowledge about time was derived only from the light and dark hours. The meaning of

---

[7]Westermann, Claus, *Genesis 1-11, A Commentary,* p. 112.

[8]Ps. 104:2, Eastern Aramaic text, Errico translation.

[9]Errico, Rocco A.,*The Mysteries of Creation: The Genesis Story,* "The Literary Pattern," pp. 94-96.

"day" as we now understand it was unknown at that early time. The calendar was not known, and the sun, moon, and stars were not created. Therefore the term "day" must not be considered a twenty four hour period.

The Aramaic word for "day" is *yauma*; and the word for the sun is *shimsha*. (Whenever Near Easterners swore by the sun, they would look up to the sky, stretch forth their hand, and say: "By that *yauma*, I am innocent.") At this particular epoch in history, the calculation of time was different; that is, a *yauma* or *shimsha* might have meant long segments or periods of time.

Many teachers of religion believe that the term "day" in this verse means a twenty-four hour period, but this could not be so because the sun, moon, and stars were not created until the fourth day. Evidently, the human concept of the scientific calendar came much later.

Time is not absolute. It is relative. Nowhere in Scripture do we read that God created time, but we do read that God created the sun, moon, and stars so that time could be calculated.

DARKNESS

Darkness is temporal and unreal and is merely the shadow of the earth. There is always the sun and light above the earth. And since darkness is relevant to the rotation of the earth, it cannot exist in the mind of God. But it does exist in the human mind. Therefore, humans saw the difference between the light and the darkness. God sees nothing but light. Darkness has no existence in the realm of the spirit. Again, darkness is relative to the position of the earth with respect to the sun.

Light is symbolic of truth and understanding; darkness is symbolic of ignorance and misunderstanding. Through enlightenment and God's constant divine revelation and guidance, humanity became aware of its creator and finally of its own spiritual self and relation to the unseen presence called God.

Darkness or harmful thinking and actions still dominate the

human mind and obscure its understanding of the creator and the vast universe in which people live. But in due time, darkness or misleading forces will be conquered by God's light; that is, humanity will come to understand spiritual energies that dwell in people and in the universe.

EVENING AND MORNING

The phrase "And the evening and the morning were the first day"does not mean a twenty-four hour period. This is because there can be no dawn or dusk without the sun. The writer used the phrase to determine a segment of time. Years later, hours, minutes, and seconds were revealed to people by Chaldean savants. In the book of the Psalms we read: "Day after day utters speech, and night after night shows knowledge."[10] The psalmist uses poetic, figurative speech. Again, the first chapter of Genesis is a prose poem employing figurative speech.

Firmament

And God made the firmament, and divided the waters which were under the firmament from the waters which were above the firmament: and it was so. Gen. 1:7.

Water in the firmament is thinner or finer than the denser water in the seas. This division is only relevant to the human mind and sight. God's work was always perfect but difficult to understand; however, the human quest for knowledge has revealed many of its secrets. Humans are children of God, made in the divine image and likeness; therefore, humans have power to analyze and understand all things. Knowledge comes from God; that is, God works through human beings.

---

[10]Ps. 19:2, Lamsa translation.

Vegetation, Seeds, and Trees

And God said, Let the earth bring forth grass, the herb yielding seed, and the fruit tree yielding fruit after his kind, whose seed is in itself, upon the earth: and it was so. Gen. 1:11.

According to the biblical epic, vegetation, plants, and trees were created before the seeds. The plants and trees grow and reach perfection so that they may develop and produce seeds. Plants and trees are more or less finite, but the seeds are infinite.

A small seed contains all the secrets of the plants and trees, their color and their design, in a manner that cannot be explained nor seen by microscopes. The creative germ or pattern in seeds is just as secretive and unknown as the creative spark in human beings.

Also, a seed can be kept for a long time and then planted and it will produce. Moreover, seeds know how to harness the sun's rays, work with water and soil, and bore into rocks.

Time and Seasons

And God said, Let there be lights in the firmament of the heaven to divide the day from the night; and let them be for signs, and for seasons, and for days, and years. Gen. 1:14.

Prior to the creation of the heavens and earth, time was nonexistent. Without the creation of the heavens and earth there would have been no events, no periods, no phases of the moon whereby one could calculate time. Time and space came into existence during creation.

Time, days, and years were made for man's convenience. "A thousand years in thy sight are but as yesterday when it is past, and as a watch in the night."[11] In other words, God, being from everlasting to everlasting, is not subject to time and space.

---

[11]Ps. 90:4, K. J. V.

The term *zawneh*, "seasons," here literally means "a period of time." It is time in the sense of "a while." It also can mean "an age, epoch, era." *Athwatha*, in Aramaic "signs," refers to the stars and planets that stand in the sky like landmarks on the earth. These "signs" acted as a map for the travelers in the Near East. (It is said the Chaldeans traveled during the night and slept during the day because of the intense heat of the day. They had to study the course of the stars and planets so that they could travel at night. And the gospel of Matthew reports that a star went before the magi,[12] but this really means that the magi followed the course of the stars.[13])

Shnah, "year," is a unit of time. The root of the word here means "the change from one period or season to another." According to the Hebrew calendar, a day is the period from one sunset to the next. Undoubtedly, this division of time was made after the sun was created and its movements studied by the ancients. According to the writer, all of God's work was finished in six days.

(Note that the week is not mentioned in this account of creation. Weeks and other subdivisions in time were made later. Night watches and hours were not known until day and night were further divided and our first calendar was instituted. The first mention of a smaller unit of time occurs in the Bible during the reign of King Ahaz. It was known as a degree on the sundial.[14] The term *shaa*, "hour," first occurs in the book of Daniel 3:6.)

Seasons were familiar to people from the very beginning, just as they are familiar today to primitive tribal people and to illiterate nomads who have little or no knowledge of calendars. They rely on the seasons to mark the passage of time.

The sun, moon, and stars were created for days, months, and seasons, but it took humankind a long time to discover their movements. It took savants of the ancient world many centuries before they

---

[12]Mt. 2:2, 9.

[13]See Errico & Lamsa, *Aramaic Light on the Gospel of Matthew*, "Following the Star," pp. 25-27.

[14]2 Ki. 20:10.

15

discovered that the sun is the center of this planetary system. In the ninth century CE, an Assyrian bishop, Mar Eshak, in his writings warned Christians against the teaching of the Chaldean astrologers, who correctly taught that the sun is the center. In ancient biblical days, the Hebrews believed the earth was the center.

Divisions in the Sky

And God set them in the firmament of the heaven to give light upon the earth. And to rule over the day and over the night, and to divide the light from the darkness, and God saw that it was good. Gen. 1:17-18.

All these divisions exist only in the human mind. As humankind grew in wisdom and understanding, people began to comprehend the nature of the forces around them, including the purpose of their creation. But in their studies and sciences about God's creations or works, they understood everything in relation to themselves.

For example, humans often think of darkness as an evil. But in reality, it is only during the dark hours of the night that one can find rest from the toils of the day and can see the glorious works of God, the stars, and planets. In the realm of the spirit, all things are good because they all exist of necessity. There is nothing in creation that is maleficent in and of itself. It depends on how humans relate to it.

Dragons or Sea Monsters

And God created great whales, and every living creature that moveth which the waters brought forth abundantly, after their kind, and every winged fowl after his kind: and God saw that it was good. Gen. 1:21.

Literally, the Aramaic text reads: *wawra alaha taneeneh rawbeh,*

"And created God huge dragons"[15] The Aramaic word *taneeneh*, in Hebrew *taneeneem,* also means "sea-dragons, sea-monsters, serpents, whales, crocodiles, hippopotami." Early in Israel's history *taneen* was the mythical monster of chaos. The term later became a general reference for huge sea creatures. It also refers to the northern constellation Draco, part of which forms a semicircle around the little dipper.

Again, the Torah writer of creation makes a simple statement. The *taneeneh* are nothing more than huge water animals—sea creatures. They are no longer a representation of ancient divinities. Hebrew, Egyptian, Canaanite, and Mesopotamian legends refer to different primeval gods or monsters, such as the Dragon, Leviathan, Behemoth, the Flying Serpent, the Twisting Serpent, the Crooked Serpent, and many other monsters. In various passages of Scripture, however, they are nothing more than prosaic comparisons of evil.[16] Biblical sages and prophets also refer poetically to these sea monsters.

Metaphorically, the term *taneeneem* means "devil, evil." Likewise, the Aramaic word *leviathan* metaphorically means "anything wicked, evil, and devilish."

Humankind

And God said, Let us make man in our image, after our likeness: and let them have dominion over the fish of the sea, and over the fowl of the air, and over the cattle, and over all the earth, and over every creeping thing that creepeth upon the earth. Gen. 1:26.

The Aramaic text reads: "Then God exclaimed: Let us make humankind in our image, as our resemblance! And they will rule over the fish of the sea, and over the flying creatures of the sky, and over the animals, and over all the wild land beasts, and over all the reptiles

---

[15]Eastern Aramaic Peshitta text, Errico.
[16]Job 7:12, 40:15, 41:1, Isa. 27:1, 51:9-10; Ps. 74:13-14.

that creep on the earth!"[17]

GOD IS ONE

According to the biblical text, Moses told the Israelites that God is one. This oneness of God had preserved the religion of Israel and unified the Israelites against much opposition and persecution.

In Near Eastern countries, kings, bishops, princes, high ecclesiastic officials, and governmental authorities must use the plural form when speaking of themselves. In the Near East, the "us, we, our" form of speech is referred to as "the plural of respect." It is never used by common folk unless the person means him/or herself with others.[18]

This form of speech has been a stumbling block to many Western readers and scholars of Scripture, especially if they are unfamiliar with Semitic culture and mannerisms of speech. It has led some to believe that there are three gods and not one. Others say there are three persons who make one God. Such a concept of God, especially when making God plural, was and is totally alien and repulsive to Near Easterners and to the Jewish people who taught vehemently against such a doctrine.

The doctrine of the trinity was introduced during the Nicean council in 325 CE. Before this time, both Christians and Jews understood God as one and not in three persons. Neither the prophets, Jesus, nor his apostles ever attempted to explain the Godhead.

Prior to the conversion of the emperor Constantine, all Roman emperors were worshiped as gods. The emperor, empress, and crown prince constituted the council of state. Emperor Gallicus was the last pagan Roman ruler who demanded to be worshiped as a god. Any

---

[17]Gen. 1:26, Eastern Aramaic Peshitta text, Errico.

[18]Western scholars refer to the plural form of speaking as "the plural of deliberation." This style of speech occurs in self-deliberation. Usually the grammatical cohortative begins with the plural and ends with the singular. See 2 Sam. 24:14 and Gen. 11: 7-8. Also Umberto Cassuto refers to it as "the plural of exhortation." See U. Cassuto, *A Commentary on the Book of Genesis:* Part One, From Adam to Noah, pp. 55-56.

18

person who refused to accept his divinity was exiled or put to death.

Seemingly, it was difficult for the pagan world to comprehend the Semitic concept of one God. The ancient church of the East still maintains that there is only one God with three attributes.

IMAGE

The Aramaic word *Nasha*, "man, human being, mortal," derives from the word *nishma*, "breath;" "living being," that is, the breath of life. Only in spirituality and eternalness is *nasha*, "man," the image and likeness of God. That is, the breath of God, being spiritual and eternal, makes a human being spiritual and eternal.

God does not create anything opposite or contrary to its own nature. God has no hands, feet, or eyes. God is not flesh; neither does God sleep or walk as is often portrayed. Humans often reduce God to human terms so that they may understand invisible spiritual forces.

God is spirit and is all-knowing, all-hearing, all-seeing. Therefore humans know, hear, and see because of the eternal spirit of God which dwells in humanity. A physical being knows nothing more than its own image and likeness, but a spiritual being is constantly conscious of its own spiritual likeness and greatness.

Literally, the word "image," *salma*, means "statue, idol." The word "likeness" refers to resemblance. This is not to be understood literally; what the writer reveals is that humanity is to be respected as God's image and resemblance. Truly, God is imageless, intangible, and invisible. How can one describe the unknown? One has to use what is known in order to explain the unknown. A human being is the tangible, visible image of God. This does not imply that God is a corporeal being. The "image and likeness" is characterized by intelligence and knowledge. The earthy, physical image of humanity is temporal and mortal, but the Spirit of God is immortal and real and is the integral essence of humankind. Moreover, a human is conscious of a Creator and knows the difference between good and evil. None of God's other creatures are endowed with this knowledge, nor are they governed by moral law.

19

Humans, being the image and likeness of God, have power and dominion over all of God's creations. What the inspired poet and writer sees by declaring humans as God's image is the unique position and relationship humans have with the transcendental—that is, God. It is a highly dignified declaration of the value of a human being, especially in relation to the creator. It is true that humans are akin to animals and can be extremely vulnerable and excessive in violence and injurious behavior. Nonetheless, the creation writer is fully aware of the total capacity of a human being, the spiritual essence of all humanity.

Adam

So God created man in his own image, in the image of God created he him; male and female created he them. Gen. 1:27.

Adam signifies "red soil," pointing to the idea that a human is related to the earth. The root of the word means "red, blood, ruddy, ruby." The word for the soil or ground in Hebrew is *adamah.* This implies that "Adam" was of the red earth, ground, or soil—an earthling.

According to the first chapter of Genesis, however, both male and female were created spiritually by God just as God had created all other things. The spiritual beingness of humanity was not formed out of the dust of the ground. For verses twenty-six and twenty-seven reads: "God created man in his own image. . . male and female created he them."

The creation of humankind took place on the sixth day, and everything was perfect and good. In other words, humankind was the last of the creations of God. Blessings were bestowed upon humanity, and God told them to multiply and rule over all creations. Thus, the first chapter gives us a picture of creation and God as Creator. Here God gives commands, and everything is done according to divine will; whereas, in the second chapter God works with human hands like a man.

The second account of creation is a commentary on the first chapter. Dr. Lamsa suggests that chapter two is the work of a later scribe, who tried to explain the creation of humanity in a symbolic, figurative manner so that people might understand what had happened. This second narrative of creation is also old and has a spiritual value. It was placed next to the first chapter simply because it is an explanation.

Some people believe that the second account of creation contradicts the first one. But this is not so. The second one was written from a human point of view. The first creation writing is spiritual; therefore, God works as God and not as a human. In the second story, God acts as a human, creating from the ground and molding man like a potter creates vessels.

The reader must remember that the Bible is a library containing extensive material that was written at various times by different authors. No inspired Hebrew writer could have thought of God literally mixing soil and forming a human being out of it. Nonetheless, Hebrew prophets and biblical authors often portrayed God as a human being planting vineyards or trees and doing other manual work.

Seeds

And God said, Behold, I have given you every herb bearing seed, which is upon the face of all the earth, and every tree, in the which is the fruit of a tree yielding seed; to you it shall be for meat. Gen. 1:29.

Plants and their seeds were created on the third day. But humans were created on the sixth day. The green herbs and fruit-bearing trees were created for food. Pristine humans lived on plants and fruits.

God had given authority to humans to rule over the beasts, birds, and creeping things, but people first derived their sustenance from vegetables and fruits. Eating meat came much later, probably when

21

people's need for food increased or perhaps from famine.

Later, every moving thing that lives was given for food. (See Genesis 9:3-4.) Interestingly, in Genesis 3:21, we read that God made skin garments, and with them God clothed the man and woman. The skins might have been the skins of sheep that were slain for food.

However that may have been, according to the narrative Adam and his wife ate vegetables and fruits at first. Many varieties of edible herbs and fruit trees grow in the region of the Garden of Eden north of Mosul, Iraq. Most of the seeds of the trees and vegetables were carried by the Roman armies to Europe from the Garden of Eden.

CHAPTER 2

Understanding the Second Creation Narrative

The second and third chapters of Genesis that narrate the second creation epic do not contradict the first episode of creation. Rather these chapters are an explanation or a commentary on the first chapter. The first creation episode is chapter 1:1-31 and chapter 2:1-3. The fourth verse of the second chapter is a transitory verse leading into the second creation narrative.

The first account is a metaphysical approach to creation. It is a spiritual revelation. God acts and creates like a supreme Deity, commanding everything into existence. Spiritual and metaphysical ideas are like liquids and gases. And just as one needs containers to transport these substances, so it is with spiritual concepts. In the Near East, abstract spiritual and metaphysical truths are illustrated in poems, parables, allegories, and metaphors. These are the containers that carry and communicate spiritual verities.

This is the only way to convey a spiritual idea of God and creation to simple folk living in desert lands, who have heard about the seas but never seen one, who have eaten fruit, but some of whom have never seen the trees on which it grows. How can one lecture to a desert tribe about a ship without drawing a picture of it and making a small sea to show it floating on the water?

Biblical authors often portrayed God taking on earthly tasks just like a human being. In these passages of Scripture, therefore, God plants a garden eastward in Eden for himself,[1] mixes clay like a potter, forming a man and animals out of the soil. Next God acts as a midwife, breathing the breath of life into the nostrils of the clay figure of a man for animation,[2] and then performs an operation like

---

[1]Gen. 2:8.
[2]Gen. 2:7 and 2:19.

a surgeon, removing Adam's rib and creating a woman from it.[3] Finally, the Lord God makes clothing out of animal skins for the Edenic couple like a tailor.[4]

If one thinks that both creation episodes of Genesis are the work of the same author and that both are spiritual revelations, then the second record of creation, chapters two and three, does seem to contradict the first account.

Sixth Day—Not Seventh

And on the seventh day God ended his work which he had made; and he rested on the seventh day from all his work which he had made. Gen. 2:2.

The Aramaic text reads: "And on the sixth day God finished his works which he had made; and he rested on the seventh day from all his works which he had made."[5]

The Aramaic word "sixth" is confused with "seventh." Had God finished his work on the seventh day, then God would have been working on that day—that is, Saturday. But God finished all the work on the sixth day, Friday; therefore, he rested on the seventh day and blessed it because all work was completed.

The writer of Genesis tells us: "So God blessed the seventh day, and sanctified it; because in it he had rested from all his works which God created and made."[6] "Rested" in this verse means "ceased." God was not tired of working, but the work was completed.

The Sabbath begins at 6:00 p.m. on Friday evening.[7] Israelites worked six days, but according to Mosaic law, they rested from their

---

[3]Gen. 2:21-22.
[4]Gen. 3:21.
[5]Gen. 2:2, Eastern Aramaic Peshitta text, Lamsa translation.
[6]Gen. 2:3, Eastern Aramaic Peshitta text, Lamsa translation.
[7]See Lk. 23:54 and Jn. 19:31.

work on the seventh. "Six days you shall do your work, and on the seventh day you shall rest. . ."[8] "For in six days the Lord made heaven and earth, the seas, and all things that are in them, and rested on the seventh day."[9] "Remember the Sabbath day, to keep it holy."[10]

As one can see from holy Scripture, no portion of God's work was left to be done on the seventh day. The completion of the work was on the sixth day.[11]

God Blessed the Seventh Day

And God blessed the seventh day, and sanctified it: because that in it he had rested from all his work which God created and made. Gen. 2:3.

Some Near Eastern commentators state that God blessed the seventh day simply because God did not work on that day. The other days were blessed by the work of divine commands. Therefore, Israel observed the seventh day because God ceased from working and sanctified that last day. According to the author, the seventh day is to be put aside as a holy day wherein all may rest from their work and worship their creator.

All days of the week are holy, but the Sabbath day was declared to be the most holy because God ceased commanding and creating on that day. During the course of time, the Sabbath came to be the most important institution in the Jewish religion. Commentaries upon commentaries were written on its observances. Years later it became

---

[8]Ex. 23:12, Eastern Aramaic Peshitta text, Lamsa translation.

[9]Ex. 20:11, Eastern Aramaic Peshitta text, Lamsa translation.

[10]Ex. 20:8, Eastern Aramaic Peshitta text, Lamsa translation.

[11]The Aramaic text is not the only text that uses the "sixth day." The Samaritan and Septuagint versions also read "sixth" instead of "seventh." Did translators of these three versions from Hebrew deliberately make this change? Or did an original Hebrew text also read "sixth day"? Scholars disagree on this issue. However, a strong preference exists among Jewish interpreters in favor of the Hebrew Masoretic text reading of "seventh day."

so sacred that even works of mercy, such as the practice of healing, were questioned.[12] Jesus of Nazareth taught that the Sabbath was made for the sake of man and not man for the sake of the Sabbath.[13]

The Term "Lord God"

And every plant of the field before it was in the earth. And every herb of the field before it grew; for the Lord God had not caused it to rain upon the earth, and there was not a man to till the ground. Gen. 2:5.

The Hebrew Masoretic text reads, *YHWH ELOHIM,* translated as "Lord God." The Aramaic Peshitta text reads, *MARIAH ALAHA,* also "Lord God." But the actual Hebrew name of God is *YHWH.* "And the Lord spoke with Moses and said to him: I am the Lord *(YHWH).* I appeared to Abraham, Isaac, and Jacob as God *(El),* the almighty God (El Shaddai); but the name of Lord *(YHWH)* I did not make known to them."[14] In the ancient days God was known as *El*–אל. In the first chapter of Genesis the author uses the Hebrew term *Elohim*–אלה ים, in Aramaic *Alaha*–אלהא.[15]

YHWH derives from the Hebrew verb *hayah,* "to be." This name suggests the eternal God as the essence of all life and existence. The term *YHWH* became so holy that Israel never dared to pronounce it. The Israelites substituted another term for *YHWH;* they used *Adonai,* which means "Lord." This is why all translations use the term "Lord God" instead of *YHWH* God. No one really knows how to pronounce it. Scholars suggest *Yahweh,* but no one knows for certain.

The Hebrew patriarchs referred to God as *El.* Jacob renamed the town of Luz, which was in Canaan, *Bethel,* meaning "the house of God." *Elohim* is a later name and is a plural form of *El.* The Hebrews,

---

[12]See Lk. 13:14.

[13]See Mk. 2:27.

[14]Ex. 6:2-3, Eastern Aramaic Peshitta text, Errico. I transliterated the names of God from Hebrew and not Aramaic.

[15]When reading Aramaic and Hebrew, read from right to left.

during the time of the conquest of Canaan, believed in the existence of other gods, but they maintained that *YHWH* was the God of gods.[16] "God standeth in the congregation of the mighty; he judgeth among the gods."[17] (Aramaic text: "He judges among the angels.")

Time after time, the people of Israel lost their pure concept of monotheism and worshiped other gods. But their prophets constantly fought against their reversion to idolatry.

Mist

But there went up a mist from the earth, and watered the whole face of the ground. Gen. 2:6.

The Aramaic text reads: "But a powerful spring gushed out of the earth and watered all the face of the ground."[18] Many lands in the Near East are watered by a mist or *telala* (Hebrew: *tal*).The lands of Canaan, Moab, Ammon, and many other desert lands depended on the dew that appeared in the early morning for irrigation.[19]

This chapter is the result of man's study of the earth and the universe. All things were revealed in the fullness of time. The earth existed before the rivers and the brooks. Undoubtedly, the early Chaldean scientists knew that the rivers and streams were formed by the flow of waters back into the seas and oceans from which the mist rises and covers the ground. Where there is no water, there are no river beds or courses.

---

[16]See Jos. 22:22.
[17]Ps. 82:1, K. J. V.
[18]Gen. 2:6, Eastern Aramaic Peshitta text, Lamsa translation.
[19]Prov. 3:20, Zech. 8:12.

God Formed Adam

And the Lord God formed man of the dust of the ground and breathed into his nostrils the breath of life; and man became a living soul. Gen. 2:7.

The creation of man and woman is described in the first chapter of Genesis: "male and female made he them" This is recorded as the work of God by command—that is, by *El* or *Elohim,* the universal God. But in the second chapter we read about *Yahweh,* the Lord. The Hebrew patriarchs had never used this term for God. Their deity was always known as *Elohim,* or *El,* the God of Abraham, Isaac, and Jacob. This is the universal God, the creator and source of life.

But *Yahweh*, the Lord, was a tribal deity with limited powers. *Yahweh* was stronger than the lords (gods) of other tribal people and nations; but, at times, even *Yahweh* was limited to a geographical location. *Yahweh* was the Lord of the mountainous regions.

When the Israelites were in Egypt, they had lost some of the knowledge of their forefathers' God. Moses did not know the name of the deity of his people until God told him: "And God said to Moses: *"AHEEYAH ASHARA HEEYAH ."*[20] (Dr. Lamsa translates this name as "I am the Living God," that is, "the One who always has been and continues to be.")

Again, the second account of creation, chapters two and three, is based on the understanding of their tribal God, *Yahweh.* The writer portrays the *Yahweh* God as a human being limited in his powers and knowledge. God has no fingers to shape or form a person or an object. God creates by spirit and the spoken word. The reader needs to keep in mind that this episode is a commentary explaining the metaphysical first chapter of creation. The author also has God behave as a midwife blowing into the nostrils of man the breath of life, clearing the nostrils, and making the man breathe. Thus, man became a living being.

According to the first account, God had already created man and

---

[20]Ex. 3:1, Eastern Aramaic Peshitta text, Errico transliteration. See also Ex. 3:13.

woman. The author places God in the role of a potter making a clay man and, if understood literally, contradicts the divine revelation of the first account. Humankind (male and female), according to the author of chapter one, is the image and likeness of God, a spiritual image wherein is life eternal.

The Garden of Eden

And the Lord God planted a garden eastward in Eden; and there he put the man whom he had formed. Gen. 2:8.

The term Eden derives from *Edan*, "a moment," "a season," or "a time." It also means "to make pleasant, delight, temporal." Material pleasures are delightful, but they are temporal; they are only for a short span of time.

The author of Genesis locates paradise eastward in Eden between the two historic rivers, the Euphrates and Tigris. God's garden is the fertile land between these two great bodies of water in the region north of Iraq (Kurdistan) where vegetables and trees grow without being planted or cultivated. Rhubarb, asparagus, green peas, celery, tulips,[21] a kind of endive, and many other varieties of vegetables grow wild in the basins of these two great rivers. Wheat and cotton also grow in the region. Moreover, grapes, pears, apples, almonds, figs, walnuts, and many other trees are plentiful. Medicinal herbs are also collected here by both native and foreign doctors.

This is the reason the region was called Eden. The term "garden," *pardaysa* in Aramaic, derives from the Persian word *pardesa,* meaning a "park, garden." This region in northern Iraq is like paradise compared with the parched lands of Arabia, Syria, and Palestine. Water is abundant. Besides the two great rivers, there are many streams and brooks and the climate is temperate, dry, and healthful.

This area became the symbol of a delightful land abounding with

---

[21]Tulip bulbs are eaten, especially when other foods are scarce.

trees, vineyards, vegetables, and water. The Garden of Eden was also called the Garden of God because God planted the trees and vegetables and made it beautiful in every way.[22] In other words, it was exceedingly beautiful because only God could have planted such a garden.

The Trees in the Garden's Center

And out of the ground made the Lord God to grow every tree that is pleasant to the sight, and good for food; the tree of life also in the midst of the garden, and the tree of knowledge of good and evil. Gen. 2:9.

THE TREE OF LIFE

In Semitic languages, trees are often symbolic of human beings. Vines mean nations; cedars mean kings. Israel is often called a vine or a vineyard.[23] Nevertheless, these two trees are set apart and given particular names and are to be understood metaphorically. The writer is merely introducing the trees.

Some Near Eastern commentators suggest that the "tree of life" symbolically might represent man's progeny. However that may be, the clause reads: "the tree of life also in the midst [center] of the garden, and the tree of knowledge of good and evil." These two trees were different from all other trees and therefore were used metaphorically or symbolically.

As far as the narrative is concerned, the tree of life clearly reveals the fact that Adam is physical and mortal and that this tree grants life, renewal, and regeneration. He was dependent on that tree. In Near Eastern legends there was always some sort of plant or vegetation that granted life and in some cases immortality. What is not clear about the tree is how often one needs to eat of it. Could one

---

[22]Ezk. 31:9.
[23]Isa. 5:1; Mt. 21:33.

just eat of it once or did one have to eat of it continually? Nonetheless, the main idea is that this tree is connected with life. The earthling (Adam) had within his reach the possibility of eternal life.

THE TREE OF THE KNOWLEDGE OF GOOD AND EVIL

The tree of the knowledge of good and evil is a peculiar title and implies the knowing of everything—that is, a comprehensive, functional knowledge. "Good and evil" does not refer to just one aspect of life but to all existence. One gains understanding through the knowledge of the ins and outs of life. "Evil," in the case of the tree, does not necessarily or always refer to something wicked but rather to a disadvantage or to the down side of matters. In Aramaic, the word for "good" is *tawa* and "evil" is *bisha*. In the Hebrew tongue the words are *ha-tov* and *ha-ra*.

People often refer to small children as innocent because they have not obtained or developed the capacity to make sound judgments and, therefore, they are not considered responsible They do not possess a comprehensive knowledge about life. Later on in the story God forbids Adam to eat of this tree. Why? Because he was not ready to handle the power that comes from this knowledge. He was like a child, innocent, but once his eyes were open a different story was to take place in human history. This is what the storyteller teaches through this narrative.

Interpreted, the tree represents the human ability to make self-governing decisions for one's own welfare and that of others because of knowing good and evil—that is, having a comprehensive knowledge.[24] The moment we possesses this knowledge, we become accountable for our actions.

In chapter three, these trees play a major role in the narrative. This is the reason for their introduction in chapter two. (See the comment below, "The Forbidden Tree," for more insight into the

---

[24]See Sarna, Nahum M., The JPS Torah Commentary *GENESIS,* "The Tree of the Knowledge of Good and Evil," p. 19.

understanding of the tree of the knowledge of good and evil.)

Pison

The name of the first is Pison: that is it which compasseth the whole land of Havilah, where there is gold. And the gold of the land is good: there is bdellium and the onyx stone. Gen. 2:11-12.

The Aramaic reads *Pishon.* The difference here is due to the Hebrew and Aramaic languages where *sh* is often pronounced as *s.*

Havilah might be the region of the river Zab, a tributary of the Tigris. Zab means "gold." A metal called beryllium is found here. It has been wrongly translated bdellium. The error was caused by the confusion of the Semitic letters *resh – r,* ר, with *daleth – d,* ד. These two letters are almost identical. There are four rivers that merge together and become the Tigris and Euphrates.

The land of Havilah might be a region in eastern Mesopotamia or in Arabia. The author of Genesis was describing fertile areas or deltas that were suitable for human habitation. There is a river in northwestern Iraq called Peshawer.

The names of rivers, like the names of seas and cities, often change. At times, when famous cities were conquered, the conqueror gave them new names.

Gihon

And the name of the second river is Gihon: The same is it that compasseth the whole land of Ethiopia. Gen. 2: 13.

The name of the second river is Gihon. The Semitic name for Ethiopia is *Cush.* The regions of Midian and Yemen were known as *Cush.* The Ethiopians ruled southwestern Arabia for many years. Gihon might be the Nile that circles the land of Ethiopia.

However, *Cush* is mentioned in Genesis 10:8 as the father of Nimrod, whose kingdom began in Babylon, Erech, Accad (Aramaic: *Accar, Akar*), and Calmeh, in the land of Shinar. Cush might originally have been an ancient region in Assyria named after Cush, the father of Nimrod.

These rivers might be named after the original rivers in and around the garden of Eden by the people who migrated from there, as in the case of English and American cities.

Hiddekel

And the name of the third river is Hiddekel: that is, it which goeth toward the east of Assyria. And the fourth river is Euphrates. Gen. 2:14.

The Hiddekel (Aramaic: *deklat*) is another name for Tigris. *Dekleh* means "palm trees." Mesopotamia was noted for date-bearing palms. A large percentage of the regional date palms grow in Iraq.

The Garden of Eden is near the sources of the rivers Tigris and Euphrates in northern Iraq. Water is symbolic of light and life. This fertile region was the first to be populated and thus became known as the cradle of the human race. The inhabitants of this land were responsible for some of the greatest inventions—notably, the alphabet, calendar, the chariot, military organizations, and many scientific discoveries.

The author located Eden in a region where fruits and vegetables of all kinds grow wild. The mountains are graced with fruit trees, vines, green peas, rhubarb, celery, and scores of other varieties of vegetables. The climate is ideal and temperate.

Eden means "delight" or "temporal. This region is the most delightful one in that part of the world. "Paradise" is the Persian or Chaldean word for garden, or an orchard spread on the ground. Semitic Near Easterners often use the term "garden" metaphorically, referring to "a wife."[25]

Adam in the Garden of Eden

And the Lord God took the man, and put him into the garden of Eden to dress it and to keep it. And the Lord God commanded the man, saying, Of every tree of the garden thou mayest freely eat. Gen. 2:15-16.

THE GARDEN

God is now portrayed as a Near Eastern potentate who owns a beautiful garden.[26] Near Eastern kings, princes, and high officials often possess beautiful gardens of their own where they can contemplate and think over matters of state. They need someone to tend and keep their gardens. So God also has a garden, and the man made from the ground is put by God on the divine property to till and keep it.

Adam was formed elsewhere and then placed in the garden to do specific chores. He must bear the responsibility of keeping the garden in good condition. He was learning to care for the grounds and its fruitage. God also told Adam to freely eat of every tree, evidently including the tree of life in the center of the garden. However, in the next verse, Adam was commanded not to eat of the tree of the knowledge of good and evil, which was also in the center.

"The center of the garden" refers to the safest and most delightful section of a garden. In the Near East, the best trees that bear the precious fruits are planted in the center of the garden. This is done so that thieves or even travelers may not venture into the center of the garden and eat of the prize fruits; they usually take from the trees along the edges. There is also another deterrent for any would-be fruit robbers. The owner's booth is usually in the garden's center so that

---

[25]See Sol. 5:1.

[26]It is helpful to keep in mind that all of this narrative is Near Eastern metaphoric and symbolic style of storytelling should not be understood as historical fact.

he may watch over his garden or vineyard and especially when his most extraordinary trees are planted there.

SPIRITUAL COMMUNICATION

All of God's communication with Adam took place in a divine revelation or through intuition. As long as Adam followed God's guidance, he could hear and perceive every command of God.[27]

Prophets and men of God, after overcoming their physical weaknesses, communed with God by means of dreams, visions, and revelations. God spoke to Abraham, Isaac, Jacob, and Joseph in dreams and visions. "For God speaks once; he does not speak a second time; In a dream, in a vision of the night, when deep sleep falls upon men, while slumbering upon the bed; Then he opens the ears of men, and humbles them according to their rebelliousness."[28]

Throughout the Hebrew Scripture, the ideas and messages were communicated to the patriarchs and prophets through symbols and inner knowing. But in the story, Adam could hear the inner voice speaking to him, guiding and admonishing him.

The Forbidden Tree

But of the tree of the knowledge of good and evil, thou shalt not eat of it: for in the day that thou eatest thereof thou shalt surely die. Gen. 2:17.

There is no record of God creating anything evil. Nor did God create a tree with evil in it. The tree is a metaphor, a figure of speech. The first account of creation informs the reader that everything God created was exceedingly good;[29] since God is good and everything

---

[27] At that time, there was no language as we have today. All words and languages were born out of human necessities in a gradual manner. Adam intuited God's command and instructions.

[28] Job 33:14-16, Eastern Aramaic Peshitta text, Lamsa translation.

[29] Gen. 1:21.

35

that was created was good, there would be no room for evil. Saying this another way, God cannot be the author of both good and of evil.

The tree of the knowledge of good and evil, especially the phrase "good and evil," refers to uniform parts of a whole—more simply put, "everything."[30] The term "evil" is misunderstood. Another way to put this idea is knowing what is helpful and harmful, knowing the pros and cons, or having a comprehensive, functional knowledge.[31]

Evil was created through humankind's pride, rebellion, and desire for power. Human beings were created with a free will and with the ability to choose and do what is uplifting or harmful. But, according to the narrative, humans wanted to usurp God's authority and power so that they could become like the gods. Humanity was not content to occupy a second-place position.

It seems that human beings are never satisfied with their stations in life. Even when one becomes an emperor, he still craves more power and glory and wants to be worshiped as a god. According to history, many kings and emperors had proclaimed themselves deities and were worshiped by their subjects. In the ancient world, Roman emperors declared themselves to be the sons of the gods.

THOU SHALT SURELY DIE

"For in the day that thou eatest thereof thou shalt surely die." By not complying with the divine command, Adam would bring an immediate and punitive reaction. According to the narrative, both the man and woman were exiled from the garden. They transgressed the only commandment that God had given and that was to refrain from eating of the tree of the knowledge of good and evil. The only restriction placed on Adam's freedom was this tree. He had to keep himself in check and to practice self-restraint in eating fruit of the

---

[30]See comment on Gen. 2:9,"The Trees in the Center of the Garden," especially p.31, The Tree of the Knowledge of Good and Evil.

[31]See Gen. 2:9 and the above comment "The Trees in the Garden's Center," pp. 30-31.

forbidden tree. The tree was forbidden because he was not yet ready to understand the power nor bear the responsibility and accountability the tree granted.

Once the couple were exiled from the garden they lost access to the tree of life, which bestowed upon them continual renewal. Now they lost the opportunity for eternal life.[32] Their physical bodies were always mortal, temporal, and destructible. The exile brought them to the full realization of death.

Animals

And out of the ground the Lord God formed every beast of the field, and every fowl of the air; and brought them unto Adam to see what he would call them: and whatsoever Adam called every living creature, that was the name thereof. And Adam gave names to all cattle, and to the fowl of the air, and to every beast of the field; but for Adam there was not found a help meet for him. Gen. 2:19-20.

In Genesis 2:7, we read that Adam was also formed out of the ground. The term Adam means red soil. The first chapter of Genesis does not say that man was formed out of the soil. But according to the second chapter, everything comes out of the ground: trees, vegetables, animals, and mortal man. Humans were to be sustained by the food from the ground. On the other hand, the spiritual essence of a human is eternal and indestructible.

Animals have no names, but humans who communicate with a spoken language have classified them and given them names.

The narrator now prepares the reader for the introduction of a helpmate for Adam. Both of them would care for the garden. Adam would no longer be alone because he would have both the animals

---

[32]See comment "The Tree of Life," pp. 30 and 31. There existed many other ancient Near Eastern, Mesopotamian legends that relate approximately the same type of story: How man gained knowledge but lost the plant of eternal life because a serpent stole it from him.

and his woman.

Rib

And the rib, which the Lord God had taken from man, made he a woman, and brought her unto the man. Gen. 2:22.

The term "rib" metaphorically means "support, helper, one who sustains another." The woman was created as a helpmate or as an assistant; therefore, she is man's rib because man leans on her just as the human body is supported by ribs. All of these notions confirm and affirm Near Eastern culture. In the first chapter of Genesis, we are told, "male and female created he them." The only command was to be fruitful and multiply and take care of the land.

God putting Adam to sleep, performing surgery, and removing a rib are used as an explanation showing the close similarities between man and woman. They both were created by God as one and equal. Humanly speaking they are two, but spiritually they are one.

Of course, the woman is anatomically different from the man but not inferior to him. They are both the image and likeness of God. According to the narrative, the woman is to be blamed for the transgression. But in the ancient Near Eastern mind-set, women were blamed for everything. Most legends, myths, parables, and narratives of the past reflect the societal and cultural beliefs of that age.

Bones and Flesh

And Adam said, This is now bone of my bones, and flesh of my flesh: she shall be called Woman, because she was taken out of Man. Gen. 2:23.

In Aramaic, the phrase "you are now bone of my bones and flesh of my flesh" means "we are identical." In the Near Eastern culture, a person who thinks highly of another person may say: "He is my bones and my flesh." This carries the idea that the two people are one. Adam and Eve were one in every respect, but one was made male and the other female. In Hebrew the writer refers to man as *ish* and the woman *ishah,* meaning one.

In this account, however, the woman is depicted as being inferior to man and was created as a helper. The author has God creating the woman as an afterthought because he saw that Adam was lonely and needed a helper.[33] God, in these passages, does not act in omniscient ways but as a human being who comes to a certain realization after the fact. As it has been stated earlier in the comments, the second and third chapters are not a divine revelation but a metaphoric explanation and interpretation of the first account. In other words, this account is man's own idea of creation.

Loyalty to the Wife

Therefore shall a man leave his father and his mother, and shall cleave unto his wife: and they shall be one flesh. Gen. 2:24.

This verse may have been copied from a marginal note revealed to a prophet or a man of God who was a scribe. According to the story, the couple had no father or mother; therefore, the phrase was probably added as an inspirational note.

In the Near East, marginal notes are sometimes incorporated into new texts, especially if the writing is the work of a man of God. Scribes, who are the copyists, generally copy any important material that is written on the margin of the manuscript. In the early days before the scrolls were canonized, new material was inserted into the new scrolls.[34]

According to this narrative, the woman was made from the

---

[33]See Gen. 2:18.

[34]The Hebrew Scriptures were canonized at the Jewish Council of Jamnia about the end of the first century CE.

man's rib, and since she was made from his rib, they are one and not two.

Evidently, marriage was meant to be monogamous from the very beginning. Polygamy was a man-made ordinance dictated by man's physical desires, needs, and greed for power. (Jesus of Nazareth did not sanction the practice of polygamy. The prophet from Galilee said: "Have you not read, that he who made them from the beginning made them male and female? [the implication was one male and one female]"[35]).

A man must cleave to his wife, simply because it is not good that a man should be alone or take another man's wife or break up another's union. In biblical days kings, princes, and powerful men took the wives of other men by force and deserted their own wives. No matter when this verse was revealed and written, it has veracity. According to the gospels, Jesus, as a teacher of the Torah and prophets, quoted it and upheld it as an inspired passage.

Naked

And they were both naked, the man and his wife, and were not ashamed. Gen. 2:25.

At this early stage, Adam and Eve knew nothing about sin. Everything that God had created was good, and they also were good. Therefore, they had no concept of evil.

Sin, shame, and evil came as the result of transgression against God's command. As long as the divine command was not broken, sin was dormant. The man and the woman were not ashamed of anything.

This verse is also considered a transitory passage, setting the

---

[35]Mt. 19:4-6, Mk. 10:6-9. Nonetheless, there were many followers of Jesus who were married to more than one woman. The only restriction placed on them was that elders and leaders of the congregations were to have only one wife.

stage for the next episode. There is also a play on words with the Semitic term "naked" and in the first verse of chapter three, with the word "shrewd." In Hebrew the word is ערו מים–*arummim,* "naked," and in chapter three "subtle, shrewd," ערו ם–*arum.* In Aramaic it is similar, ערים–*areem.*

CHAPTER 3

A Perspective of the Third Chapter

Adam and Eve are representational of humanity and are fictional characters who have become historicized. Since the first account of creation claims that everything is good, the question arises, what has happened to humanity? Some biblical commentators suggest that the first creation story is a priestly writing depicting a world that humanity can look forward to and anticipate. The second account answers the question, in metaphoric and symbolic storytelling, of what happened, and continues to happen, to humankind.

The narrative of the transgression of Adam and Eve, their punitive consequences, and exile from paradise is the story of what humanity continually endures by constantly seeking power over others. The tree of the knowledge of good and evil represents power—that is, becoming gods. Human beings have the tendency to self aggrandizement and deifying their own powers. Knowledge bestows power. One can use it to control and manipulate or bless and advance humanity into a new state of enlightenment and understanding.

Serpent

Now the serpent was more subtle than any beast of the field which the Lord God had made. And he said unto the woman, Yea, hath God said, Ye shall not eat of every tree of the garden? Gen. 3:1.

Metaphorically, "serpent" means "a deception" It did not become connected with the term "Satan" or "devil" until the first century BCE. In the apocryphal book *Wisdom of Solomon*, the writer invents and makes a connection referring to the "serpent" as Satan: "It was the devil's [Satan] envy that brought death into the world, as those who are his partners will discover."[1] The terms "Satan" and "devil" became interchangeable. Also, the idea of comparing serpents with craftiness and deceitfulness is very old. According to Mesopotamian, Hurrian, and Ugaritic legends, serpents represented the opposition to the ancient deities. In those days, the serpent was a Canaanite fertility symbol, and in the royal house of Egypt, it was a protective emblem.

In common Aramaic speech, people often say, "he has been a snake in my house," meaning "he has been an enemy in my house." Jesus told his disciples that they would be handling serpents, meaning "the opposition and enemies to their teaching."[2] However, the term "Satan" or "devil" was not known to the early Hebrews, nor does it occur in the early books of the Hebrew Bible.

"Serpent" is symbolic of a human being's capacity for self-deception and rebellion against the Creator. Had God told the man and the woman that they must eat of the tree of the knowledge of good and evil, they probably would not have touched it because they would have wanted to rebel and disobey the divine command.

A human being is not a robot to be ordered to do things. It is a part of human nature and power to revolt. People have the freedom of choice to express what is good or what is harmful and damaging. Another way to put it: the serpent symbolizes our false idea about ourselves and about our wisdom, greatness, and creative powers. The notion here is that since Adam had been given dominion over everything, why then should he obey a power greater than himself?

The author uses the serpent because it is the most subtle and shrewd creature on earth. It takes subtleness and cleverness to deceive anyone. But no serpent is more shrewd or subtle than the human power to mentally manipulate one's self and others. It is true that humankind has dominion over all creation, and nothing from outside

---

[1]Wisdom 2:24, Jerusalem Bible. It is the Septuagint translation of this verse that renders the Hebrew word "Satan" as "devil." The author of this apocryphal book interprets the third chapter of Genesis and portrays the devil or Satan introducing death into the world.

[2]Mk. 16:18.

can force someone to behave rightly or wrongly. Therefore, a human being is free to adhere to divine guidance or oppose it.

Some interpreters of Scripture claim that the serpent was used by God as an agent to tempt Adam and Eve. If that is the case, why then did God, according to the narrative, curse the serpent for fulfilling the divine mission. On the other hand, the serpent could not have tempted Adam and Eve as a mission from God because, "Let no man say, when he is tempted, I am tempted of God; for God cannot be tempted with evil, neither does he tempt any man."[3]

Another point which is often overlooked is that although the serpent speaks directly to the woman, the man was present with her listening to their verbal exchange. How do we know this? It is because the serpent, throughout his conversation, addresses both of them. In the Hebrew and Aramaic texts, the author has the serpent use the plural pronoun "you" while speaking to Eve, which implies Adam was there. The text in English says: ". . . She gave also to her husband who was with her, and he did eat."[4]

Like Gods

And the serpent said unto the woman, Ye shall not surely die; For God doth know that in the day ye eat thereof, then your eyes shall be opened, and ye shall be as gods, knowing good and evil. Gen. 3:4-5.

The proposition of the serpent is to place doubt into the minds of the man and woman concerning the legitimacy of God's restriction. The serpent has elicited a response from the woman only; the man silently watches and listens to the suggestions. It subtly plants the notion that a higher state of existence is possible and that their creator is not to be totally trusted.

"Your eyes will be opened" means you will have greater power

---

[3]James 1:13, Eastern Aramaic Peshitta text, Lamsa translation.
[4]Gen. 3:6, Eastern Aramaic Peshitta text, Errico.

knowing the ins and outs of everything. In other words, you can live independent of God. You will become like gods, divine beings; you will have great power equal to the divine.

The suggestion has now been made and they are about to choose wrongly. Their choice is between God and knowledge that grants power. According to the story, here is the challenge for all humanity: choosing rightly or inappropriately—that is, between spiritual, inner guidance and human reasoning alone. Serpentine thought represents the human capacity for self-deception. None of this literally took place. It reveals the root of humanity's difficulties. Harmony between the creator and humans was disrupted.

Ashamed

And he said, Who told thee that thou wast naked? Hast thou eaten of the tree, whereof I commanded thee that thou shouldest not eat? And the man said, the woman whom thou gavest to be with me, she gave me of the tree, and I did eat. And the Lord God said unto the woman, What is this that thou hast done? And the woman said, The serpent beguiled me, and I did eat. Gen. 3:11-13.

In Aramaic "naked" also means "exposed." The serpent had promised Adam and Eve that when they had eaten from the fruit of the tree in the center of the garden their eyes would be open and they would become as gods, knowing the upside and downside of everything.

Up until this point in the narrative, Adam and Eve had known nothing but God. Everything that God had created around them was understood as good. But now, when they transgressed God's command, they saw the counterpart of what was called good—that is, what was not so good. Now they were naked and ashamed. Before this they were naked and saw nothing but good; they looked upon their nakedness as positive and natural. It is true their eyes were now open and saw all sides of being naked. Now they saw the negative side of their nakedness and needed to be clothed. This action gave birth to civilization—clothing.[5] Nonetheless, the breaking of any divine command brings remorse and shame.

They both had listened to the beguiling serpentine talk, which represented the opposite to God's command. Human functional knowledge is limited. Adam and Eve were not ready yet to handle the knowledge they had now gained; the insight was too much. They were to reproduce spiritually minded offspring, but by breaking the Creator's command, they set a wrong direction for humanity. Human beings usurped the right to make judgments concerning their social welfare and human well-being completely independent of divine guidance and in resistance to spiritual ways of living.

The Serpent's Penalty

And the Lord God said unto the serpent, Because thou hast done this, thou art cursed above all cattle, and above every beast of the field: upon thy belly shalt thou go, and dust shalt thou eat all the days of thy life. And I will put enmity between thee and thy woman, and between thy seed and her seed: it shall bruise thy head, and thou shalt bruise his heel.
Gen. 3:14-15.

"Serpent" in this instance means the "lie" or "deception" that brought on the opposition to divine truth. Again, the author metaphorically uses the serpent as an agent of deceit. People considered the serpent as sly and shrewd. Now the condition of the serpent was to change. The creature who had walked upright and could talk will now slither on its belly, eating dust, and suffering the loss of speech. Because the serpent had exalted itself by indirectly challenging God, it finishes in abject humiliation, which is always the result of deception. Many people fear serpents because to them they have

---

[5]The idea of needing clothes also reinforced the ancient Near Eastern cultural notion of the shame of nakedness.

become a harmful object of distaste always striking at the heels of humanity. Humanity does trample the serpent and it always strikes back. Nonetheless, there is another meaning behind this cursing of the serpent.

"And I will put enmity between you and the woman, and between your posterity and her posterity; her posterity shall tread your head under foot, and you shall strike him in his heel."[6] The offspring of the woman was to trample the serpent's head; that is, ignorance and deceit would be continually exposed. God created no evil; therefore, evil itself is a falsehood and misunderstanding of life brought on by noncompliance to divine guidance. There would be an ongoing enmity between the Spirit of truth, which also indwells humanity, and the constant striking of deceit in the hearts and minds of people. The day will come when humankind will have victory and dominion over deceptive thinking and harmful actions. A spiritual humanity will arise in triumph over the serpent. In simpler terms: wherever deception continues, its posterity will be trampled upon.

This verse has also been interpreted that a promised Messiah (an Anointed one) was to arise and crush the head of the serpent and save humanity from destructive forces, bringing people back to God. This messianic interpretation is found in late Judaism but not in the New Testament. In the Christian Church, beginning with Irenaeus up to the present, a large percentage of interpreters represent the serpent as Satan and the seed of the woman as an individual who would crush him. According to this Christological interpretation, Jesus of Nazareth as the Messiah/Christ fulfilled this role and crushed the head of the serpent.[7]

The Jewish Galilean prophet did reveal to humanity a new light of understanding and spiritual power over all harmful, abusive thinking and actions. Jesus, as one anointed by God, taught the

---

[6]Gen. 3:15, Eastern Aramaic Peshitta text, Lamsa translation.

[7]All these interpretations are rejected by modern biblical criticism, especially the approach of form-critical analysis. These biblical scholars do not understand this verse as a prophecy or a promise.

essential Torah and its life-giving truths, demonstrating it throughout his life, teaching, and healing ministry, and during his crucifixion. But it is doubtful that the narrator had this in mind when he told this story.

Multiplication of Pain Not Sorrows

Unto the woman he said, I will greatly multiply thy sorrow and thy conception; in sorrow thou shalt bring forth children; and thy desire shall be to thy husband, and he shall rule over thee. Gen. 3:16.

The Eastern Aramaic text reads, "I will greatly multiply your *pain* and conception" instead of "sorrows." The biblical narrative confirms the idea that pain, sickness, and sorrows were the result of humankind's departure from the ways of God. However, just as God did not create sin, evil, or the devil, God also is not the author of pain, sickness, and sorrows.

Any departure from truth brings suffering. Regret and grief are the usual results when something which is wrong, deceitful, and harmful is done. Just as soon as the man and the woman had transgressed God's command, they found themselves to be powerless. Before their act of defiance, they were like angels, free from physical difficulties. Now the woman was to bear children in pain.[8]

The last part of the verse in the Eastern Aramaic text reads: "And you shall be dependent on your husband, and he shall rule over you."[9] Women were completely dependent on their husbands for the provisions of food and shelter This saying mirrored the social world

---

[8]Although the storyteller believes that painful childbearing was due to disobedience, the science of biology teaches that it comes from evolutionary stages, the enlargement of the human brain and skull. Generally all other species, especially mammals do not suffer as the female humans do.

[9]Eastern Aramaic Peshitta text, Lamsa translation. Literally, however, the Aramaic text reads: "And toward your husband shall you turn and he will rule over you."

of the times. Again, the storyteller associates male dominance over the female in his society as the result of the transgression of the divine will. Before their departure from God's command, the sexes were of equal status.

Thorns and Thistles

And unto Adam he said, Because thou hast hearkened unto the voice of thy wife, and hast eaten of the tree, of which I commanded thee, saying, Thou shalt not eat of it: cursed is the ground for thy sake; in sorrow shalt thou eat of it all the days of thy life; Thorns also and thistles shall it bring forth to thee; and thou shalt eat the herb of the field. Gen. 3:17-18.

"Sorrows, thorns, and thistles" in Semitic languages mean great difficulties and grievances. Working the ground with much labor to bring forth the necessary food became for the man a challenge and a great deal of trouble. When he tended to the garden everything was provided for him, and the work was not that difficult or challenging. All he had to do was to take care of it. Constructive work is not a curse, and struggle is an elan of life. People are blessed by the work of their hands.

Work itself is not a curse. When God planted the garden in Eden, Adam was placed there to work. It was the disobedience to God's command that made working the ground outside Eden's garden extremely demanding. When sin (error) is dominant, it makes life difficult and complicated.

Human troubles are not due to labor, but rather to the material and physical concepts of life to which humanity has enslaved itself Thorns and thistles—that is, hardships in life—come about by departing from God's grace, good laws, and the true path of life.[10]

---

[10]Thorns and thistles are not a curse. Plants produce thorns for self protection. Man's involvement in working the ground, clearing the thorns and thistles, creates the difficulties. In the ancient world, it was very challenging. Also bramble bushes, thorn bushes, created a problem with the sheep when they became caught in them.

"And thou shalt eat the herb of the field." For a second time the command is given that humanity shall eat of the vegetation of the land. (A reiteration of Genesis 1:29: "And God said, Behold I have given you every herb yielding seed, which is upon the face of the earth and every tree which bears fruit yielding seed; to you it shall be for food.") Farming was understood as humankind's first or earliest occupation.

Interestingly, a plant is one of the greatest marvels on earth. It stores the sun's energies and converts it into food for itself, for birds, fish, animals, and humans. All life is sustained by it. Plants are very old and very wise. They were created before humankind. In the book of Daniel, we read that Daniel had stopped eating meat and called for vegetables and by so doing his wisdom became superior to all other wazirs of Babylon.

Return to the Ground

In the sweat of thy face shalt thou eat bread, till thou return unto the ground; for out of it wast thou taken: for dust thou art, and unto dust shalt thou return. Gen. 3:19.

"In the sweat of thy face shalt thou eat bread" is an Aramaic idiom signifying "bearing up under much hardship." Again, this is a repeat of the Semitic figures of speech, "sorrows, thorns, and thistles." All these Near Eastern expressions, including "sweat," mean life will present many difficulties and grievances. The sentence takes on an ironic twist. Adam and Eve were supposed to become like gods; instead they are now faced with the vulnerability of life and the hard struggle to maintain their lives. They lost their consciousness of abundant living.

"For dust thou art, and unto dust shalt thou return" refers to the death of the human being, who is mortal. According to the second chapter, which is based on symbolism and figurative speech, the human, Adam, was formed out of the ground and to the ground (soil) he was to return. This is because that which comes from the ground is earthy and must return to the earth. But this pronouncement has nothing to do with the spiritual being created in the image and likeness of God.

In the original account of creation, Genesis 1:1 to 2:3, man was not created out of the ground but directly from the Spirit of God; therefore, the spirit must return to God who gave it. "Then the dust shall return to the earth as it was; and the spirit shall return to God who gave it."[11]

According to the storyteller, returning to dust was a part of the punitive action for breaking trust with God's command. Humans were to bring forth a perfect and spiritual creation. Now the couple were left to rely on their own knowledge and to work their own salvation. Their transgression brought a heavy penalty.

Coats of Skin

Unto Adam also and to his wife did the Lord God make coats of skins, and clothed them. Gen. 3:21.

Now that Adam and his wife have come to a realization that nakedness holds a sense of shame for them, God helps them adapt to their new condition and makes coats of skin. Their former dignity is restored by God because he provided clothes for them. They also will need these clothes for living outside God's paradise.

In the beginning, seemingly, humankind may have gone without clothes like all of God's creatures. However, they also might have had longer hair on their bodies than people have today. Apparently, after wearing clothes, human bodily hair may have gradually diminished. But as far as the narrative is concerned, Adam and Eve were innocent until their eyes were opened and were not ashamed of any members of their body and their functions.

---

[11]Eccl. 12:7, Eastern Aramaic Peshitta text, Lamsa translation.

When they broke God's command and became knowledgeable of both sides of everything, they discovered their nakedness and became ashamed and afraid of God. They covered themselves with the large Mesopotamian fig leaves. And when the Lord God saw that they were hiding their nakedness, especially their genitals, God asked them who had told them that they were naked. After they confessed, the Lord God showed them that they must cover themselves with the skins of sheep and goats.

According to the biblical narrator, the Lord God made them clothing like a tailor.[12] This means that God gave them an idea to clothe themselves with better material than fig leaves. This incident hints that humans may have been eating the flesh of animals already. In the first chapter, God never commanded man to slay animals for food. They were living on herbs, seeds, fruits, and vegetables.

Become as One of Us

And the Lord God said, Behold, the man is become as one of us, to know good and evil: and now, lest he put forth his hand, and take also of the tree of life, and eat and live for ever: Therefore, the Lord God sent him forth from the garden of Eden, to till the ground from whence he was taken. So he drove out the man: and he placed at the east of the garden of Eden cherubims, and a flaming sword which turned every way to keep the way

---

[12]For many centuries, skins of animals were the only apparel known to humankind. In some European countries, cloth was unknown; even the kings and princes of Europe were clothed in animal skins, such as ermine, the skins of foxes and other wild animals. Weaving was introduced into Europe by the Arabs when they conquered Spain. Prior to that time, cloth was imported from Mosul, Iraq, Egypt, and Lebanon. All kings' apparel came from Lebanon.

In Babylon the history of weaving is very old. During the time of Joshua, Ackar stole a beautiful, expensive Babylonian woven tapestry. He was put to death by Joshua. Weaving began in Mesopotamia because cotton grew wild everywhere. Also, the palm and date trees contained a cloth-like burlap that nature wove in order to protect the tender shoots. Humanity learned many things from nature and from the trees, birds, and animals.

of the tree of life. Gen. 3:22-24.

When the serpent (deceptive thoughts and mistrust) caused Adam and his wife to transgress, the serpent promised them that if they ate from the tree that was in the center of the garden, they would not die, but instead they would be as gods, knowing good and evil. In other words, they would become powerful.

This was a lie. They would not become divine beings. The only thing they would come to know was functional knowledge. (Undoubtedly, had the serpent's promise been true, he would have eaten from the tree himself.)

God's utterance, "Behold, the man is become as one of us," is used sarcastically and demeaningly, mimicking the lying words of the serpent. God knew that the fruit from the forbidden tree could not make the couple rivals or gods. God quoted the serpent's words to expose his lie, as if to say, "see, you didn't become gods."

Adam and Eve were assured by the serpent that if they ate from that particular tree in the center of the garden, they would know everything. The truth is that God would not have created such a tree nor have been jealous of man who would become divine. Again, humans were created in the image and likeness of God. They already possessed a divine and spiritual nature.

What happened was this: Notions of grandeur and power were put in the minds of the couple by the serpent—that is, their own deceptive forms of thinking. According to many Jewish legends that developed later, the serpent, which became known as the devil, became jealous of man because man was created in the image of God and had dominion over all creation.

Evil has no origin. The serpent was used allegorically. Human capacity for self-deception is responsible for creating evil and harmful acts against itself and others. Only truth and understanding can conquer the roots of evil.

CHERUBIM

Angel, *malakha,* in Aramaic, means "messenger" and implies God's counsel or message. The term "Cherubim" in Aramaic is *k'rowa* and in Hebrew is *k'rubim.* These Cherubim had specific functions differing from other angels who carried only messages from the divine. Cherubim functioned as guardians and protectors. In the ancient Near Eastern world, the images of Cherubim were placed on the thrones of kings as symbols of protection. They had human heads and bodies with wings on their backs. They also carried spears and swords.

Moses placed the Cherubim over the ark of the covenant,[13] forming the mercy seat where God's voice was heard. These images were to put fear in the minds and hearts of anyone who would dare touch or attempt to steal from the ark. The curtains in the tabernacle of God had graphic representations of Cherubim, signifying divine presence and protection. These curtains separated the two inner chambers—the holy of holies (innermost compartment) from the holy place. Only the High Priest was allowed to enter the Holy of Holies once a year, on the Day of Atonement. Moses entered whenever he was guided or needed to commune with God. Cherubim also decorated the highly stylized temple of Solomon.

Ezekiel, in his vision, described the Cherubim as having four heads (man, ox, eagle, and lion) with six wings and carrying the platform upon which was God's throne. Each head represented the powers and strength of God. They appear once again in the book of the Revelation.[14]

These creatures symbolized God's omnipresence and divine sovereignty. However, Cherubim are not to be understood literally; they are symbols. They are not heavenly or earthly creatures. They derive from Near Eastern imagination meant to describe in the known

---

[13] Hebrew Sacred Chest wherein were the tablets of the Commandments, manna, and Aaron's budded rod. The ark resided in the Holy of Holies.

[14] See Rev. 4:6-8.

symbols of the times the spiritual reality of God.

After God had exiled the couple from the garden ("drove them out"), God placed the Cherubim on the East of the garden of Eden. As a separate symbol from the Cherubim was the image of the flaming sword to guard the path to the tree of life. The flaming sword served as a protection because God said, "and now lest he put forth his hand, and take also of the tree of life, and eat, and live forever." Again, all of this is symbolic and describes the state or condition of all humanity.

Interestingly, in ancient Israelite symbolism, the Cherubim also represent protective winds. And the "flaming sword which turned every way" refers to lightning flashes that appear in a cloud like a sword. Lightning creates fearful streaks of flame and fire which turn in diverse directions. This would make it impossible for the human couple to return and access the tree of life.

Nevertheless, in the book of the Revelation, the tree of life is mentioned one more time. Access to the tree is granted by God's Spirit to those who conquer their evils and lust for power. "He who has ears to hear, let him hear what the Spirit says to the churches [congregations]: to him who overcomes; I will give to eat of the tree of life, which is in the midst of the paradise of my God."[15] In addition to this verse in Revelation, according to John's gospel, the teaching of Jesus of Nazareth opens the way to eternal life for humanity.

Concluding Remarks

The Garden of Eden episode is a Semitic story and tradition. Other races also have their own traditional stories of how humanity appeared on the earth. This biblical allegory or parable was to affirm a truth that all peoples on earth are of one origin and are all children

---

[15]Rev. 2:7, Eastern Aramaic Peshitta text, Lamsa translation. See also Errico and Lamsa, *Aramaic Light on James through Revelation,* "Part 2, The Tree of Life," p. 109.

of the same God. This is what made this traditional narrative so much more outstanding than any other Near Eastern tradition.

There are basically three interpretations attempting to explain the Garden of Eden narrative: (1) Sexual, (2) Ethical, and (3) Intellectual. Sexual interpretation is based on the Hebrew word for "knowledge," which implies sexual experience. Then the notion of nakedness and sexual experience is connected with shame. Ethical interpretation refers to humanity's awakening to moral discrimination and finding itself capable cf sinning. Being put out of the garden and forever being barred from reentry means that humanity could never return to its former self of ethical indifference; humanity now has to choose. Intellectual interpretation refers to the human awakening of knowing what is good and what is bad, therefore attempting to know everything and become god-like—that is, Omniscient. None of these interpretations were employed in the above commentary.

The major point to keep in mind is that the story is not to be understood as actual history. Regardless of how one may interpret the episode, God, Adam, Eve, and the serpent all play a role in this drama of the human condition. The meaning is simple: every human being is always faced with either following the inner, spiritual guidance or following the outward appearances of things (symbolized by the tree of the knowledge of good and evil) and thereby gaining power. "You will be like gods" is humankind's strong desire for power to control and manipulate others. According to the biblical epic, humans were granted power over the animals and the earth but not over other members of the human family. All humanity was to be guided by God—Love, Peace, and Harmony—and they were to do good works.

CHAPTER 4

Cain

And Adam knew Eve his wife; and she conceived and bare Cain, and said, I have gotten a man from the Lord. And she again bare his brother Abel. And Abel was a keeper of sheep but Cain was a tiller of the ground. Gen. 4:1-2.

The Aramaic text reads: "And Adam had sexual intercourse with Eve [Aramaic: *Hawa*], his wife." *Hkam* in Aramaic means "to know, discern, to have sexual intercourse." In Hebrew the root is *yd* and has a very wide range of meanings; it does not necessarily carry the idea of only knowing something intellectually. It connotes knowing relationally, emotionally, neurologically, and experientially. In other words, this kind of knowing involves the entire physical being.[1]

Cain (Aramaic: *Qaein*) derives from the Aramaic root *qana,* "to gain, acquire." The birth of the first child was a gain to Adam and Eve after the heavy loss and disgrace they had suffered in the garden of Eden. According to Chapters 2 and 3 of the second creation narrative, the woman came from the man, and now a man-child comes from the woman. Eve gained a man from the Lord. Ancient Semites believed that it took three to produce another human being—God, a man, and a woman.

Eve's second son was named Abel (Aramaic: *Habel*), meaning "nothingness" or "a loss." Either an inner voice told his parents what would happen to Abel, or he was given this name at his death. Adam and Eve suffered another loss.

In the Near East, generally, when a man has two sons, the

---

[1] Most biblical scholars, both Jewish and Christian, understand that this was not the first time that the couple had physical relations. It is based on the use of the verb "to know" in the pluperfect. They had experienced coition when living in the garden of Eden before they ate of the forbidden tree. See also Gen. 3:20.

younger one usually tends to the sheep and the older works in the field raising food for the family. Cain followed the same occupation as his father. Adam had worked the ground in the garden, and now he tilled the ground outside the borders of the garden of Eden. It was natural for Cain and Abel to have diverse lines of work, one being a shepherd and the other a farmer.

The First Offerings to God

And in process of time it came to pass, that Cain brought of the fruit of the ground an offering unto the Lord. And Abel, he also brought of the firstlings of his flock and of the fat thereof. And the Lord had respect unto Abel and to his offering: But unto Cain and to his offering he had not respect. And Cain was very wroth, and his countenance fell. Gen 4:3-5.

This is the first mention of an offering made to God. Since Genesis was written many centuries later, the idea of this first offering to God must have been handed down orally from father to son. Because writing was unknown at that time, many other biblical narratives were handed down orally.

We must also understand that this episode about God being displeased with Cain's offering is once again a story that had been in circulation by word of mouth for a very long time. Many elements were left out when it finally was recorded. God is no respecter of persons and, as a loving Father, cannot be partial to anyone.

Both brothers offered what was within the reach of their hands. But Cain, most likely, did not present his offering from a true, inner devotion to God. In his heart Cain was rebellious. He was the first offspring of Adam and Eve after they had transgressed God's guidance. Evidently, Cain harbored a brooding, moody demeanor.

What one offers to God does not matter. But what one offers wholeheartedly does. Most of the Hebrew prophets declared that what God wants is a pure, sincere heart, compassionate and just. The narrative hints at some negative characteristics and behaviors

58

practiced by Cain.

As far as the animal sacrifices that Abel brought, God takes no pleasure in animal or meat offerings. Again, it depends on the sincerity of the individual. However it is the storyteller that has God being pleased and displeased. It is based on the culture of the times. On the other hand, Near Eastern religious men prefer sheep, rams, and he-goats as offerings. They shun wheat, cheese, and other offerings that are difficult to maintain and keep.

Near Easterners praise the man who proffers meat offerings. They love broiled meat, but they do not care much for cereal food. Some interpreters suggest that the rejection of the produce might be a priestly theory. But this is doubtful.

Cain Warned by God

If thou doest well, shalt thou not be accepted? And if thou doest not well, sin lieth at the door: and unto thee shall be his desire, and thou shalt rule over him. Gen 4:7.

The Aramaic text reads: "Behold, if you do well, shall you not be accepted? And if you do not well, sin lies at the door. You should return to your brother, and he shall be subject to you."[2]

Cain was jealous and envious not only because his brother's offering was accepted but probably because Abel was a kinder and more just man. Apparently there existed a strong rivalry and envy between the older brother and his younger brother. Rivalry between brothers is a common theme throughout Scripture. This is also well illustrated in the parable of the prodigal son.

Cain probably harbored a grudge against his brother. Abel was seemingly more sincere and upright in heart and mind than Cain. According to the narrative, God warns Cain that his grudge and jealousy were dangerous and would soon erupt in a crime. "Sin lieth

---

[2]Gen. 4:7, Eastern Aramaic Peshitta text, Lamsa translation.

at the door" means that the passion to commit murder was apparent in Cain's demeanor. But if Cain would have made peace with his brother, Abel would have been subject to him as the rightful heir and ruler of the family. Cain refused to listen to God's admonition and was determined to rid himself of his brother by slaying him.

Cain's Fear and His Mark

Behold, thou hast driven me out this day from the face of the earth; and from thy face shall I be hid; and I shall be a fugitive and a vagabond in the earth; and it shall come to pass, that everyone that findeth me shall slay me. And the Lord said unto him, Therefore whoever slayeth Cain, vengeance shall be taken on him sevenfold. And the Lord set a mark upon Cain, lest any finding him should kill him. Gen. 4:14-15.

Cain's fear of being slain raises the question whether there were other people besides the Edenic couple. Those who maintain that the Eden narrative is allegorical believe that there must have been other people dwelling in the territory besides Adam and his family.

According to the narrative, there were only four persons in existence—namely, Adam, Eve, Cain, and Seth. And yet, after Cain had slain his brother and the Lord drove him out from before the divine presence, Cain was afraid to go into the land of Nod. He was fearing that someone might slay him. Some biblical interpreters maintain that had there been no other people, Cain would not have been afraid, and no one would have found him and slain him.[3]

It is maintained that there were other people east of the river Tigris. The land of Nod in Aramaic means "the land of the wandering tribes." Persia (Iran) was noted for its wandering tribes, the Lors and the Bakhtiari. In the Near East, there still remain some nomadic people who live in tents and wander in search of grass for their large

---

[3]Other biblical interpreters suggest that Cain was referring to the future offspring of his parents and that they would want to exact revenge on Cain.

flocks. But this has greatly diminished and is becoming extremely rare.

However this may be, Cain, because of the fear of being killed, asked for God's protection. The last portion of the verse clearly reveals that Cain was afraid that he might be slain in the land of Nod.

Cain had a guilty conscience. He had taken the life of his own brother. Now he was afraid that the blood of his brother would be avenged upon him. He knew that whoever sheds another man's blood, by men shall his blood be shed.[4]

THE MARK OF CAIN

Up until the late 1940s, murderers were branded in biblical lands. The mark bore witness that the individual had been punished for his crime.

Cain knew God was exiling him from his homeland and thus he would become a wanderer like a Bedouin and certain Iranian tribes. He wanted some sort of protection. In the Near East, when a man flees his country and takes refuge among strange peoples and lands, everyone wants to know why. Any person who leaves his kinsman, traditions, and religion comes under a great deal of suspicion. They will think of him as an outlaw and he will not be welcomed into the community. Cain wanted assurance from the Lord that he would not be put to death. Cain was exiled from the region around Eden and the mark was the evidence that he had been punished. God assured Cain that anyone who would slay him would be punished sevenfold.

SEVENFOLD

Biblical authors frequently used the number seven because they believed it was a holy number. It symbolized the seven known planets of the ancient world and the seven stems of the Jewish lampstand known as the menorah. Because of the constant usage of the number

---

[4]See Gen. 9:6.

seven, Near Easterners could relate to it.

Cain Takes a Wife

And Cain went out from the presence of the Lord, and dwelt in the land of Nod, on the east of Eden. And Cain knew his wife; and she conceived, and bare Enoch: and he builded a city, and called the name of the city, after the name of his son, Enoch. Gen. 4:16-17.

Some Near Eastern biblical scholars maintain that Cain might have married his sister. Others say Cain married in the land of Nod. The author of the narrative does not offer any answers. The whole scene of the second creation story is the Garden of Eden. There is no mention in Genesis that Adam and Eve had any daughters. If not, then Cain must have married a woman from the land of Nod (Persia), or God might have provided a wife for him just as God did for Adam.

However the original story might have been, Cain was married. Where he was married and to whom is irrelevant. The author of the narrative does not explain how Cain obtained his wife, but simply says that Cain knew his wife. But there is a hint that there were other people.

When Cain left the Edenic region that was between the rivers Tigris and Euphrates, he crossed the Tigris into what we call Iran and there he married and begot children. His descendants were noted for their large flocks of cattle. Cain was the father of the roaming tribes who dwell in tents and tend large flocks and herds.[5]

The term "Persian" also means "wanderer," the people who spread out and live in tents, moving from one place to another, seeking places to graze and water for their livestock. In Aramaic, the Persians are called *Mbadreh*, "the scattered people." Years ago, many of them lived the tribal life as they did in the past.

_____

[5]Gen. 4:20.

The Eastern Aramaic text reads: "He started to build a village and named the village after the name of his son Enoch."[6] Enoch means "rest." This is the first village that was built by the descendants of Cain. Up until this time, Cain and his descendants had been wandering, but now they began to build a village and engage in agriculture, just as the members of some of the nomad tribes used to do. Cain had become a fugitive and wanderer. He was also told by God that the ground would no longer yield its strength for him. But now, in the land of Nod, it changed.

The term "city" is not accurate. The dwelling place that Cain was building was no more than a small hamlet to protect him and his family during the winter and the rainy season. In those days, villages and cities were called by the names of the patriarchs and founders of the tribes or one of their sons.

Cain alone could not have built a city. What would one lone man and his wife do with a city, or even a village? Either there were other people in Nod who received Cain as a prince and helped him build a village, or his descendants, centuries after him, built a city and called it after the name of his son Enoch.

Music

And Adah bare Jabal: he was the father of such as dwell in tents, and of such as have cattle. And his brother's name was Jubal: he was the father of all such as handle the harp and organ. Gen. 4:20-21.

Jabal (Aramaic and Hebrew: *Yabal*, "moving") is the Arabic word for "mountain." The nomad tribes in Iran graze in the mountains and highlands during the summer. Mountain people are noted for their large flocks of sheep, goats, and cattle.

---

[6]Gen. 4:17b, Eastern Aramaic Peshitta text, Lamsa translation.

Jubal (Aramaic and Hebrew: *Yubal*) means "to play on a musical instrument." Cain's descendants were the inventors of musical instruments. These instruments were used to frighten wild beasts and snakes and to charm and quiet the sheep. This ancient custom still prevails among the few nomad shepherds in biblical lands.

The Tragic Story of Lamech

And Lamech said unto his wives, Adah and Zilah, hear my voice; ye wives of Lamech, hearken unto my speech: for I have slain a man to my wounding; and a young man to my hurt. If Cain shall be avenged sevenfold, truly Lamech seventy and sevenfold. Gen. 4:23-24.

This episode is an ancient footnote. The scribe of the book of Genesis included it in the text just as many other marginal notes were included and made an integral part of the Scriptures.

There is a very old Eastern tale connected with Lamech and some Near Eastern commentators explain it in this manner:

Lamech was a great hunter until the day he became blind. After he became blind, Lamech still continued to hunt. One day, he took a boy with him to help direct his bow. But on that day, he accidently killed a man. When they boy informed Lamech of the incident, he lamented. In demonstrating his great remorse over the horrible occurrence, he struck his hands together very forcefully and unknowingly struck the boy's head between his huge hands. Hence his song of lamentation that was recorded in these passages.

However the original story may have happened, Lamech had done something wrong. His guilt was greater than Cain's. He had killed a man and a boy.

Calling on the Name of the Lord

And to Seth, to him also there was born a son; and he called his name

Enos: then began men to call upon the name of the Lord. Gen. 4:26.

"Call upon the name of the Lord" has two meanings. The descendants of Seth began to identify themselves with God; that is, they began naming their children with the name of God—*El*. For example, Mahalale*el*, Methusa*el*, and Mehuja*el*. Also they began calling on God in prayer.

Seth's descendants separated themselves from the descendants of Cain. They began to trace their origin back to God, in whose image and likeness they were created. They were discovering their spiritual heritage and sonship, whereas the descendants of Cain continued to part from God's ways and to forget their spiritual heritage.

CHAPTER 5

God Took Him

And Enoch walked with God: and he was not for God took him.
Gen. 5:24.

"Enoch walked with God" means he lived a just life and followed divine guidance throughout his daily living. He was a good and righteous man with a heart and mind full of faith. Enoch was truly a man of God.

"God took him" is an Aramaic idiom meaning "he died." In Aramaic and other Near Eastern languages, the word "death" is repulsive because it denotes the end of life. People often say, "He is at rest" or "He sleeps." When a king, prince, or holy man dies, Near Easterners say: "God has taken him." Since Enoch was a holy and good man, "God took him."

"He was not" means he was no longer physically present. Being a pious man, he died physically but his soul returned to God, his creator. Enoch pleased God, died a peaceful death, and his soul lives forever.

In the New Testament, the author of the epistle to the Hebrews states that by faith Enoch was taken up and did not taste death. He was not found because God took him.[1] This is a Semitic idiomatic style of speech. In other words, he did not taste death like others. Nonetheless, some biblical interpreters believe that Enoch was taken bodily into heaven. The gospel of John states that no one has gone to heaven except Jesus Christ, who came from heaven.[2]

---

[1]Heb. 11:5.The majority of modern New Testament scholars do not accept the idea that Paul wrote the letter to the Hebrews. Be that as it may, the message about Enoch's faith is mentioned in this epistle.

[2]Jn. 3:13.

CHAPTER 6

Descendants of Seth

That the sons of God saw the daughters of men that they were fair; and they took them wives of all which they chose. Gen. 6:2.

The term "sons of God" in Aramaic means "good people," "God-like people," or "people who worship one God and do good works." The reference here is to the descendants of Seth, the third son of Adam and Eve. Prior to the flood, all the descendants of Seth were good, pious people. But when they began to intermarry with the daughters of men—that is, the descendants of Cain—they forsook God's ways.

Humanity was created in the image and likeness of God, and as long as people remained good, they were referred to as children of God. But when these people went astray, following other deities and marrying women who believed in those gods and goddesses, they slowly began to lose their heritage and realization of their divine, spiritual relationship.

Centuries afterward, the original understanding of divine sonship was regained through the teaching of Jesus of Nazareth. "But to those who received him, to them he gave the right to become sons of God, especially to those who believed in his name."[1] It is through him and the practice of his teaching that human beings once again are called children of God and heirs to God's kingdom.

---

[1] Jn. 1:12, Eastern Aramaic Peshitta text, Errico. "Those who believed in his name" is an Aramaic manner of speech, meaning that those who accepted his teaching and practiced it would express true divine sonship.

The Age of Man Reduced

And the Lord said, My spirit shall not always strive with man, for that he also is flesh: yet his days shall be an hundred and twenty years. Gen. 6:3.

"My spirit shall not always strive with man" is an Aramaic idiom that means, "I have become weary and impatient with man." This originally was a scribal note that became a part of the text. God never becomes weary, sorry, impatient, repentant, or changeable. God is omniscient, and divine laws are from everlasting to everlasting and unchangeable.

"For that he also is flesh" refers to the fact that humans, although they are the image and likeness of God, still live in the flesh and are weak; therefore, they are subject to frailty and falsehood.

Humankind's span of life or age shrank simply because a new calendar was developed by the Chaldeans, a calendar that was based on the solar system of 365 days. Before this time, the age of people was computed by the lunar or the seasonal calendars.[2] These were the first two measuring sticks of time prior to the present calendar that was developed before the birth of Abraham.

The reader must keep in mind that all these stories were handed down orally from one generation to another before the calendar and alphabet were devised. Then again, the world in which the patriarchs lived was a small world surrounded by seemingly limitless space devoid of borders and boundaries. Human concepts of time was in its infancy. It is true that God had created the sun, moon, and stars for light and for signs and seasons, days, and years. But it took a long time before human beings became familiar with the movement of the heavenly bodies.

Ancient Near Eastern authors wrote that it was a necessity for

---

[2]Each new moon or season was computed as a year but not the present way of reckoning a year. The ages of so many of the ancient patriarchs in Chapter 5 are based on the seasonal or lunar calendars.

those who traveled at night to study with the naked eye the movements of the stars and planets. (In these lands, night travel was preferable. The intense heat of the day made it extremely difficult to travel then.) According to these ancient writers, the phenomenon of night travel brought about the Chaldean development of the yearly calendar of 365 days.

Evidently, the ages of some of the early patriarchs were based on the lunar calendar and others on the seasonal calendar. In those very early days, a month was reckoned as a year. Tribal people still use the phases of the moon and seasons for grazing, planting, travel, and business.

According to Scripture, we are told that Israel had an ecclesiastic calendar of seven weeks of 150 days. Some Near Eastern Jews and Muslims still employ the lunar calendar in their worship.

Again, the phrase that God became impatient with humans was a footnote or marginal notation by a scribe when he saw that the age of men had declined so suddenly as though something cataclysmic had happened. The discrepancy between the ages of the early patriarchs and those who came later may have caused the scribe to believe that God had changed his mind and then reduced man's age to 70, 80, 100, and 120. Again, this marginal notation was copied later into the integral portion of the Bible. As is the Near Eastern custom today, many interesting marginal notes are incorporated into the main body of the writing by the copyist. Since writing material was scarce, notes were written on the margins of scrolls.

Undoubtedly, the change in the calendar changed man's concept of time. If we were to divide the ages of some of the men who had lived 800 or 900 years by 12, we would find that they lived to 75 or 80 years. And by dividing the ages of those who lived 300 to 500 by the four seasons, we would discover that they lived a normal span of life, a few living to a 120 or 125.

The reader must remember that all the books of the Bible were not written at the same time, nor were all people using a standard calendar. Some of the books were written before humanity's scientific knowledge was developed.

Giants

There were giants in the earth in those days; and also after that when the sons of God came in unto the daughters of men, and they bare children to them; the same became mighty men which were of old, men of renown. Gen. 6:4.

The Aramaic word is *ganbareh* (pronounced *"gabareh"*). The letter "n" is occulted. It means "mighty men, giants, heroes, champions." There still exist in our present world men who are extremely tall and strong. In the ancient days, these men were called *ganbareh*, "giants" or "mighty men." In the Near East and in Africa, there are many men who are of great stature and physically strong. They are so powerful that they can wrestle with an ox or buffalo and defeat it. Some of these men can even stop a car.

Dr. Lamsa recalls that in the town of Kudshanis in Kurdistan, the See of the patriarch of the Church of the East, there used to be a family whose entire household were all *ganbareh*, giants. These giants were killed by the Kurds in World War I. These men could lift huge boulders and heavy burdens without any effort or struggle.[3] Throughout Scripture, there are references to giants—that is, men of great height and strength. Samson was one of these men.

Again, the term "sons of God" refers to the descendants of Seth who intermarried with the daughters of Cain. Their offspring became very strong, valiant, and widely acclaimed.

The Impending Deluge

And it repented the Lord that he had made man on the earth, and it grieved him at his heart. And the Lord said, I will destroy man whom I have created from the face of the earth; both man, and beast, and the creeping thing, and the fowls of the air; for it repenteth me that I have made them.

---

[3]Dr. Lamsa, on one occasion, actually saw the sister of these giant men lift a tray containing five Mausers with one arm and with utter ease.

But Noah found grace in the eyes of the Lord. . . .The earth also was corrupt before God; and the earth was filled with violence. And God looked upon the earth, and, behold, it was corrupt; for all flesh had corrupted his way upon the earth. And God said unto Noah. The end of all flesh is come before me; for the earth is filled with violence through them; and, behold, I will destroy them with the earth. Make thee an ark . . . Gen. 6:6-9, 11-14a.

The biblical author tells a regrettable story of humanity's corruption and violent actions in that region of the Near East. He portrays God as being sorry and repentant for having made human beings. God, of course, is truly transcendent, but here he is described like another human being, who becomes sorrowful and grieved to his heart at the way in which humans became so violent.

The writer interprets the coming deluge as a part of the divine plan to remedy the situation by destroying every living thing except for Noah and his family so that humans may begin all over again with a renewed life.

God appeared to Noah in a dream and warned him of the terrible flood. He received the complete instructions on building an ark for his family, livestock, and other animals of the region.[4]

---

[4]See Chapter 7, "The Flood," pp. 72-74.

CHAPTER 7

Two Pairs of Animals

There went in two and two unto Noah into the ark, the male and the female, as God had commanded Noah. Gen. 7:9.

Noah saved pairs of animals that were found in Assyria (Mesopotamia). He could not have gone to China, Japan, India, or other far off lands to save a male and female of each species of animal.

Noah, like the early patriarchs, had been a sheep and cattle breeder. He had to save species of animals on which he and his family depended for food and clothing, and also some unclean animals and reptiles.[1] In verse two of Chapter 7, the writer informs the reader that Noah was commanded to take seven of the clean beasts and two of the unclean.

The discrepancy between the two accounts, the two and seven, was due either to two early oral narratives or to two early written documents. Verses 15 and 16 confirm that Noah took two and two instead of seven and seven. The most important idea is that the reader understands that Noah saved the animals for his sons and their descendants. Noah obeyed the divine voice and faithfully carried out all of God's commands; thereby, he and his family were spared.

The Flood

And the waters prevailed, and were increased greatly upon the earth; and the ark went upon the face of the waters. And the waters prevailed exceedingly upon the earth, and all the high hills, that were under the whole heaven, were covered. Fifteen cubits upward did the waters prevail; and the mountains were covered. Gen. 7:18-20.

---

[1]See Lev. 11.

The Aramaic word *araa* means "the earth, a country, land, field, region, soil, floor (of a house)." Semites generally use the term *tabel* when speaking of the whole habitable earth.

In the days of Noah most parts of the world that we know today were unknown. The land between the Tigris and Euphrates rivers was the only world that Noah and his people knew. Not for a very long time were Canaan and other westward lands fully inhabited. According to the biblical narrator, this took place only after the dispersion and the division of the languages.[2]

The Aramaic word *shmaya*, "heaven, heavens," also means "sky, skies." No doubt the hills in the region where Noah made the ark were covered with water by the flood. The deluge was so great that it lasted forty days and forty nights. The Tigris and Zab rivers flooded all the inhabited regions of the area.

"The mountains under all the heaven" would not include the Himalayas. Had the water risen fifteen cubits above the earth's highest mountains, the surface of the ocean would have risen 30,000 feet above its present level. If this were the case, the water could not have receded in one hundred and fifty days. There would have been no place for it to flow.

A similar phrase appears in the book of Numbers when Balak, king of Moab, sent messengers to Balaam, the son of Beor, and said: "Behold there is a people come out from Egypt: behold they cover the face of the earth."[3] "Face of the earth" means the face (surface) of the ground near the land of Moab. (The word translated as "earth" should read "ground." "*Araa*" is the Aramaic word in the text.)

Many believe that the narrative of the building of the ark is true because pitch and gopher wood are found in that area of Assyria. However that may have been, if all the water in the earth's atmosphere were to fall on the earth at once, the surface of the ocean would not rise more than a few inches. Of course, God can do anything, but the reader needs to realize that these early writers lived

---

[2]Gen. 11:1-6.
[3]Num. 22:5, K. J V.

in a much smaller world.

Later on in the narrative, one reads that a dove brought an olive branch back to the ark, proving that some of the mountains were not inundated. No olive trees could have survived one hundred and fifty days under the salty seawater. No vegetation could thrive when the ocean water mixed with the heavy downpour of rain water. There are many olive trees in northern Mesopotamia (Iraq) and this is where the dove obtained the branch to bring to Noah and his family.

CHAPTER 8

Mountains of Kardu

And the ark rested in the seventh month, on the seventeenth day of the month, upon the mountains of Ararat. Gen. 8:4.

The Eastern Aramaic text reads, *toorai kardo,* "the mountains of Kardu," Kurdistan. This chain of mountain ranges begins in northern Mesopotamia and reaches as far as the Armenian border near the Taurus range.

Mount Ararat is the highest mountain in the whole range of mountains in Kurdistan and Armenia. Apparently, the name Ararat was used by the translator of the Bible simply because the entire chain is identified with it. The ark rested on one of the lower mountains east or west of the Tigris, near the small river Zab and not on mount Ararat itself.

Mount Ararat is about 18,000 feet high and difficult to descend from its peak. How could Noah have brought down animals such as elephants, camels, and other large beasts when even expert mountain climbers cannot ascend or descend Ararat with proper equipment for mountain climbing. Noah and his family had their small livestock.

There is no reason to think that God would have made the ark to rest on the peak of such a high and cold mountain where neither people nor animals could descend without some disaster occurring.

God does not do something that would work against the divine purpose of saving Noah and his family. Mount Ararat, because of its height, was known to Westerners, but the mountains in Iraq where the ark was built were unknown.

Olives Not Destroyed

And the dove came in to him in the evening, and lo, in her mouth was an olive leaf pluckt off: so Noah knew that the waters were abated from off the earth. Gen. 8:11.

Had the whole world been inundated with flood waters, the trees would have perished. Ocean water would have mixed with the fresh water and the topsoil would have been destroyed. And if Mount Ararat had been completely covered by the deluge, where would the dove have found the branch with the green leaf? No olive trees grow in Armenia. But olive trees do grow in Mesopotamia. Therefore, the ark must have rested on one of the lower mountain ranges, north of the region where Noah was living, and the olive branch was picked up from a region where the olive trees were not covered with water.

Seasons

While the earth remaineth, seed-time and harvest, and cold and heat, and summer and winter, and day and night shall not cease. Gen. 8:22.

Seasons in the region of Eden are very evident. The climate is temperate and changes four times during the year. The changes from one season to another are very pronounced and the weather is not erratic. Both farmers and shepherds know the exact day of the beginning of each season.

Prior to the development of the calendar and the division of time into years, months, days, and hours, the knowledge of time was based on the changes of the season. That is, the seasons served as a calendar. This verse is the first reference in the Bible to cold and heat and to summer and winter.

The year of 360 days was divided into four seasons of three months each. Three hundred and sixty days can easily be divided into four quarters of 90 days each. Then again, the moon was a great help. Priests and shepherds were guided by the phases of the moon and the farmers by the seasons.

There are about 30 days in each moon, but for two days the moon

76

cannot be seen with the naked eye. The thirty days multiplied by twelve will give us exactly 360 days. The five extra days caused errors in the calendar that were later corrected. Early peoples did not know that the earth makes one complete revolution around the sun in 365 and 1/4 days.

CHAPTER 9

Animals Given for Food

Every moving thing that liveth shall be meat for you; even as the green herb have I given you all things. Gen. 9:3.

Seemingly, the commandment was given later when the need for food had increased. The green herb was given for food in the beginning.[1] Originally human beings subsisted on green herbs or vegetables. The grass, herbs, and the fruit trees were created on the third day, but the living creatures and the animals were created on the fifth day, before humans were created.

Like the animals, early man evidently lived on the vegetables and fruits that grew around him. Many varieties of vegetables and fruit trees grow wild in northern Iraq. This is the reason that the author of Genesis calls that region "the Garden of Eden," which means "a delightful garden." This area is truly graced with all varieties of vegetables, fruit trees, cotton, and wheat.

Some people believe that the animals that thrive on the grass are stronger than the wild beasts that live on meat.

Eating of Blood Forbidden

But flesh with the life thereof, which is the blood thereof, shall ye not eat. Gen. 9:4.

For many centuries, the Hebrews thought that life was centered in the blood. Four centuries after Abraham, blood was forbidden to be eaten as food by an ordinance of Moses. "Moreover, you shall eat

---

[1]Gen. 1:29.

no manner of blood."[2]

This is also the reason that blood was used for the atonement of sins. A sinner was cleansed by means of animal blood offered on his behalf. The author of the book of Hebrews in the New Testament, following the Mosaic idea of blood sacrifice, writes: "For if the blood of bulls and of goats, and the ashes of an heifer sprinkling the unclean, sanctifieth to the purifying of the flesh; how much more shall the blood of Christ. . ."[3]

Many people of different faiths, including some Christians, eat blood, but the Jews still uphold the Mosaic ordinance and abstain from eating meat with blood. They eat kosher—that is, clean meat without blood. The Mosaic ordinance was based on God's command that was recorded in this verse.

Vengeance

Whoso sheddeth man's blood, by man shall his blood be shed: for in the image of God made he man. Gen. 9:6.

When a man slays another man he commits a crime not only against himself but also against all humanity, because all human beings were created in the image of God. According to the biblical creation prose poem, God created one man and one woman only.[4] Therefore, when a man kills another human being, he destroys himself.[5] This is the reason the Torah declares that he who slays a man shall surely be put to death.[6] "Whosoever killeth any person, the murderer shall be put to death by the mouth of witnesses."[7]

Life is sacred because man is the image and likeness of God. So

---

[2]Lev. 7:26, K. J. V.
[3]Heb. 9:13-14.
[4]Gen. 1:27.
[5]Mt. 26:52.
[6]Ex. 21:12.
[7]Num. 35:30, K. J. V.

he who destroys a branch of a tree, destroys a part of the tree's system of life. All humanity is like one tree that shares in the same one sap of life. God commanded humanity to be fruitful and multiply upon the earth. Thus, any act that reverses the divine plan is contrary to God's order. It is contrary to the life force. The offender, through his disobedience and evil act, cuts himself off from the land of the living and the shared essence of life.

Ham

And the sons of Noah that went forth of the ark, were Shem, and Ham, and Japheth: and Ham is the father of Canaan. These are the three sons of Noah: and of them was the whole earth overspread. Gen. 9:18-19.

"Ham" derives from the Aramaic word *homa,* meaning "heat, sultriness." All three sons of Noah were of the same complexion and all of them were living in Bethnahrin (Mesopotamia). After the deluge and settling in the land, none of Noah's sons migrated from his homeland to far off lands. Assyria was large and fertile enough for all three men, their families, and flocks to dwell in the same region.

In those early days, roads were unknown and forests were infested with snakes and wild animals. Noah's sons divided the land in which they were living among themselves. Each one of them started grazing in different directions. Japheth went northward; Shem, being the firstborn, stayed home in Assyria; Ham went southward, grazing and multiplying. The ancient custom still prevails. When a large tribe splits, its segments move in different directions.

As the tribes continued to migrate they multiplied and again divided, seeking new grazing lands. When the Hamite tribe migrated southward they found more favorable grazing conditions and water, and the climate was warmer. It took many centuries before the descendants of Ham reached the hot region of Africa where, because of climate conditions, their skin became dark. Their bodies created the darker pigments to protect their skin from the strong and penetrating rays of the sun. Today, the Ethiopians are called *Amharik,* "the scorched people." This was due to the regional climate—that is, the burning rays of the sun.

When traveling from the north to the south toward Africa, one notices the skin color of people changing gradually; for example, the Arabs in the north are lighter than those in the south. And the southern Arabs are much lighter than Arabs and other races in Africa. This is also true of the Teutonic people, such as the Germans, British, Swedish, and especially Norwegians. They are very white simply because the suns's rays in the north are more indirect and not as strong. Frenchmen who live in southern France are darker than those in the north. This is also true of the Italians.

Some Bible teachers wrongly believe that it was because of the curse that Noah pronounced on Ham's son, Canaan, that he and his descendants turned black.[8] Canaan was to be the lowest of slaves to his brothers. No curse can change the skin color of a man, but heat and cold can cause changes over a period of time in the human body. And no curse can make a man a slave. Nor did Noah mention anything about cursing the color of the skin.

In the past, unfortunately, tribes who were not vigorous enough to combat the stronger and more dominant clans were made slaves by those more powerful tribal people and nations. Slavery was not due to any curse but to a manmade institution. Any tribal people who dominated the land had the tendency to make slaves of other peoples and tribes regardless of their skin color. Later, powerful nations began to make slaves from the population of the nations that they had conquered.

Wine

And Noah began to be an husbandman and he planted a vineyard: and he drank of the wine, and was drunken; and he was uncovered within his

---

[8]Gen. 9:25.

tent. Gen. 9:20-21.

Vineyards existed before the time of Noah; therefore, there was wine. The history of wine is as old as the history of religion. People discovered that when grapes were left in a container, they would ferment, and when people ate the fermented grapes with its juices, they felt the effects of the new drink. Wine was used for feasts and weddings.

In the ancient Near East, grape juice was unknown. People drank wine in moderation. The term wine is used in many books in the Bible. Noah, on this occasion, drank wine excessively, became drunk, and laid down naked on the floor of his tent. Some Bible teachers think that Noah drank grape juice, but the juice of grapes alone cannot create a drunken state.

In the story of Lot and his two daughters, Lot was given wine by his daughters to seduce him to sleep with them so that they could raise an heir for him. Had Lot not been drunk, he would not have had intercourse with his daughters.[9] (The reader must also keep in mind that the narratives of Lot and his two daughters and of Noah's drunken state, nudity, Ham's not covering his father's nakedness, and the curse placed upon Ham's son, Canaan, are allegories—that is, not historical events.)

Isaiah tells us that the princes, prophets, and priests also had overindulged not only with wine, but with strong drink (strong alcoholic beverages).[10] Paul, in his epistles, writes that whoremongers and drunkards shall not enter the kingdom of heaven. All prophets were against excessive drinking of wine and strong drink. Had people been satisfied with just eating grapes and not drinking anything strong, there would be no words for wine or drunkenness. Moses commanded that there should be no drinking while serving in the holy tabernacle.[11]

---

[9]Gen. 19:30-38.
[10]Isa. 28:7.
[11]Lev. 10:9.

Wine constituted a part of religious ritual both in paganism and in Judaism for special holy feast days. People carried wine with them when they went to celebrate and worship. They would eat, drink, and dance. When Eli saw Hannah making supplication before the Lord God, he mistook her for a woman who was drunk. "And Eli said unto her, how long wilt thou be drunken? Put away thy wine from thee."[12]

Noah's Curse

And Noah awoke from his wine, and knew what his younger son had done unto him; and he said: Cursed be Canaan; a servant of servants shall he be unto his brethren. Gen. 9:24-25.

People bring curses and destruction upon themselves. Nonetheless, ancient peoples believed in curses and blessings that were pronounced by holy men, priests, and patriarchs. God, the source of love and compassion, would not sanction or back up Noah's curse on any of his sons. The story is to be understood as an allegory.

In the Near East, the greatest curse is when one person curses the son, the heir of another, or his descendants. To just pronounce a curse directly on a man that one wishes to bring down would not be powerful or damaging enough. But to utter a curse on his son carries more weight and is more effective.

For example, Job declared that the lamp of the wicked be put out. This is metaphoric speech. The lamp means an heir. So the heirs of wicked people should be cut off from the land of living and no longer continue the evil of their forefathers. David thanked God for giving him a lamp—that is, his heir, Solomon. An heir is more important than the father. Near Easterners still curse in this manner. A Near Eastern father, while lamenting over the death of his son, will say: "I wish I were dead instead of you, my son."[13]

---

[12]1 Sam. 1:14, K. J. V.
[13]See 2 Sam. 18:33.

The shameful and disgraceful act of Ham was this: He did not cover his father when he was inebriated and lying naked on the floor of the tent.[14] Not only this, but he also reported his father's nakedness to his brothers, which also dishonored his father and compounded the offense. This was a loss of dignity for his father to be found naked and not covered immediately, especially in the Near East. His brothers entered the tent walking backwards and covered their father. By this act they restored his honor and dignity.

Some Bible teachers suggest that an act of incest was performed, but this notion is to stretch the story beyond the biblical account. There are also many other far-fetched interpretations about what Ham did to his father. There are those who even suggest castration with the help of Ham's son, Canaan. Again, in those ancient days, especially among the Hebrews, nudity was considered shameful because it demeaned human dignity. This also applies to the world of the Near East to this day.

Another point to consider in Noah's imprecation is that the curse is not really directed at Canaan himself but indirectly. "Cursed be Canaan, a servant of servants shall he be to his brethren" is a pronouncement on the people of Canaan, or rather his descendants many generations later. Ham and his son Canaan are allegorical representations of the Canaanites, who were known to the Israelites.

Ham's behavior symbolized the immoral habits of the Canaanite people.[15] These descendants were subjected to slavery and bondage not because of Ham's indecent behavior toward his father but because their own actions and transgressions were like Ham's disgraceful behavior. They lacked scruples and a strong sense of morality. Therefore, the iniquities of the Canaanites were to catch up with them, and Israel would conquer their land.

---

[14]See Hab. 2:15-16.
[15]Lev. 18:3.

Noah's Blessing

And he said, Blessed be the Lord God of Shem; and Canaan shall be his servant. God shall enlarge Japheth, and he shall dwell in the tents of Shem; and Canaan shall be his servant. Gen. 9:26-27.

Noah blessed Shem and Japheth because they had covered his nakedness. The son of Ham, Canaan, was cursed because Ham had seen Noah naked and did not cover him.

Shem was given his father's estate because he was the firstborn and heir, and Japheth was allowed to dwell among the descendants of Shem. Shem was the father of the Semitic tribes and people of the Near East, hence the term Semites (literally: Shemites).

Japheth was the father of the European races. Ham was designated as the father of black races, Egyptians, Canaanites, Ethiopians, and others.

CHAPTER 10

Magog and Meshech

The sons of Japheth: Gomer, and Magog, and Madai, and Javan, and Tubal, and Meshech, and Tiras. Gen. 10:2.

The Aramaic word *Magogh* refers to "Mongolia." Meshech or *Mashakh* refers to what is now Moscow, the capital of Russia. Gomer means "Germany;" Madai means "Media;" Javan, "Greece;" and Tubal is "Tubaliskie." Tiras is either "Tursha," one of the sea people, or "Etruscans."

The Israelites, like the Assyrians, Chaldeans, and the Persians, knew about other races and about those who were far off. The Assyrians had conquered what is known as ancient Armenia, Georgia, and other lands adjacent to Russia and the Caspian Sea. For example, Cathay (China) is mentioned in Numbers 24:24. It is also mentioned in many of the books of the prophets.

In the eight century BCE, some of the captives from the land of Israel were settled in Iran (Persia), Media, Afghanistan, and other lands in the Middle East. No doubt some of them fled to India, China, and Russia. It was during this period that the Israelites knew of these far-off places and their races.

The Arameans and the Chaldeans traded with many of the Eastern races. Their ships navigated many seas. Even today, there are large Jewish colonies in many regions of Russia and the Near, Middle, and Far East. There are also Jews of Indian origin, who were converted by the early Jewish settlers in India.

Tarshish

And the sons of Javan; Elishah, and Tarshish, Kittim, and Dodanim. Gen. 10:4.

86

Tarshish was an ancient name of a region of southwestern Spain. The region was noted for its wealth of silver, tin, and lead.[1] The inhabitants of Tarshish were the descendants of Japheth, the third son of Noah. They inhabited the region of Andalusia in southwestern Spain.

The term Tarshish is of Aramaic derivation: *tar,* "door." and *shish, (shagish),* meaning "rough, raging sea, violent." Hence, the Gibraltar, or the door to the raging, mysterious Atlantic Ocean.

Gentiles

By these were the isles of the Gentiles divided in their lands; every one after his tongue, after their families, in their nations. Gen. 10:5.

The Aramaic word for "Gentiles" is *ammeh.* It is used with various meanings; *ammeh* can also mean "kindred, races, peoples." The three sons of Noah were born of the same father and mother, and all of them and their immediate children spoke the same language. But after the dispersion, the descendants of the three sons of Noah scattered northward, southward, and eastward. And, consequently, new tribes and new languages were born.

The descendants of Laban, Lot, Ishmael, Esau (Edom), and other kindred people were called "Gentiles" by the Hebrews. Many of these people, who were the direct descendants of Abraham, revered the Lord God of Israel; in the course of time, however, most of them sank into the worship of other gods. For example, Balaam was a Gentile prophet, but he revered the Lord God, the creator of heaven and earth.[2] Laban, the Aramean, also feared the Lord God.

The Hebrew prophets predicted that the Messiah would bring the

---

[1]Jer. 10:9.
[2]Num. 22:7-14.

Gentiles to God[3] and would be a light to enlighten the Gentiles.[4] The Aramaic term *ammeh,* "Gentiles," should not be confused with pagans and Greeks.

Nimrod

And Cush begat Nimrod: he began to be a mighty one in the earth. He was a mighty hunter before the Lord : wherefore it is said, even as Nimrod the mighty hunter before the Lord. And the beginning of his kingdom was Babel, and Erech, and Accad, and Calneh, in the land of Shinar.
Gen. 10:8-10.

According to Scripture, Nimrod was a descendant of Ham, the second son of Noah. At this early time, the Hamites were of fair skin like their brethren, the Shemites. Nimrod, being a strong warrior, ruled over Mesopotamia. In those days, giants like Nimrod were feared. When a man was strong and valiant in battle, he was chosen to be the leader of the people. Also, the height of a man was considered in determining his leadership.

Evidently Nimrod was the first builder of Babylon. In his days Babylon was a little town, just as Paris and Rome were a few centuries ago. But the Assyrians enlarged and beautified Babylon and made it the capitol of all southern provinces. Isaiah states that it was Assyria that built Babylon. However that may be, Babylon played an important role in the history of the Near East as well as in the history of the Bible.

The name Accad in verse 10 is not correct. It should read "*Akhar.*" The mistake was caused by the similarity of the Aramaic letters *daleth* and *resh.* Western scholars have advanced a new hypothesis that is not mentioned in the Bible—that is, the existence of the races that they call "Accadians" and "Sumerians." There are

---

[3]Isa. 11:10.
[4]See Lk. 2:32.

88

two regions in Iraq. One is called *"Akhar"* and the other *"Shamar."* These areas were ruled by emirs or princes. The people of these regions are just like the people in Iraq and Arabia. The language and the culture are the same. All races and people have been mentioned in the Bible in one way or another. But the theory of the Summerians and Accadians is not supported by the Bible.

The term "Erech" should read *Arakh,* "Iraq." *"Arakh"* and *"Akhar"* were two kingdoms that were a part of ancient Assyria and Babylon.

In those ancient days, large fortified cities were known as kingdoms. This is why a king of Assyria, Babylonia, or Iran (Persia) was known as "King of Kings." The name Padan-Aram was changed to Assyria and later to Mesopotamia. Seemingly, the Arabs had retained the ancient name of the region, Iraq.

Amorah Not Gomorrah

And the border of the Canaanites was from Sidon, as thou comest to Gerar, and Gaza; as thou goest unto Sodom, and Gomorrah and Admah, and Zeboim, even unto Lasha. Gen. 10:19.

The Aramaic Eastern text reads *Amorah* instead of Gomorrah. Evidently, during the course of copying and translating, the Semitic letter *aey* or *ayein* was confused with the letter *gamel.* These two letters are very similar in Aramaic, especially when they are the first letter of a word. The tail of *gamal* is slightly longer than the letter *aey.*

In the Arabic language the biblical town is called *Amoriah.* The word *Amorah* means "the inhabited place." Both Sodom and Amorah were prosperous towns situated on the caravan route southeast of the Dead Sea.

Eber

And Arphaxad begat Salah; and Salah begat Eber. Gen. 10:24.

The term "Hebrew" derives from the Aramaic word *abar,* "to cross over," that is, the lands on the west side of the River Euphrates. Eber was a great-grandson of Shem, 2235 BCE. In Numbers 24:24, Eber is mentioned as a nation meaning the Hebrews. Some of the descendants of Eber remained in Haran and other places west of Assyria. Eber was the father of the Hebrews.

CHAPTER 11

The Division of Languages

And the whole earth was of one language and of one speech.
Gen. 11:1.

Undoubtedly, the ancient people who lived in the land of Shinar spoke one tongue, the first human language. The division of languages came about from the dispersion of the people from Mesopotamia. It was a slow process. It takes centuries before a new language is born or a new speech replaces an old form of communication.

According to the biblical writer, the height of the tower of Babylon created a communication problem for the builders. The structure was so high that they could not hear one another clearly. At that time, of course, elevators, telephones, and other means of communicating were unknown. The whole project of building such a high tower in Babylon was done by hand.

When a mason called for bricks, they probably sent him mortar; when he asked for mortar, they might have sent him timber. The higher the building grew the more difficult, confusing, and hopeless the task became for the builders. And when they realized that heaven was not just over the clouds and could not be reached, the builders abandoned the project and started to disperse in different directions.

In biblical days, people thought that the heavens were only a few miles above the earth. This concept still prevails among many primitive peoples who lack the knowledge of astronomy. They believe that God's abode is above the clouds. The book of Numbers informs the reader that the Lord came down in the clouds.[1] God was not afraid of man, as the biblical text may indicate. The building of the tower was an impossible project.

The dispersion was necessary because of the grazing situation

---

[1]Num. 11:25.

and the population growth. Pastoral lands were divided among the various tribes, and some of the tribes grazed southward, northward, and westward. They were in search of new pastures. Every time a tribe grew larger and became powerful, its sheep and cattle increased, and it divided itself into smaller tribes. These divisions and migrations continued for thousands of years until most of the various regions were inhabited.

It was during the course of these migrations that the new dialects were formed and later became distinct languages. At that early time, writing was unknown and commerce was in its infancy. The tribes were independent and self supporting. Every tribe, in the course of time, incorporated new words into its dialect, which became a new speech. As new discoveries were made, new words were coined.

This is also true in our day. For example, if American men and women who passed on 100 years ago would all of a sudden come back into our present age, they would find it difficult to converse with their descendants. They would hardly recognize many of our modern English words, idioms, and cultural use of words.

Even to this very day, in lands where illiteracy is predominant and where there are little social and commercial relations, people who are living only a few miles apart find it difficult to understand one another's speech. In some areas, every town has its own dialect. For example, Arabic is spoken by many Near Eastern people, but it has numerous dialects. An Arab born and reared in the Arabian desert would find it difficult and tremendously challenging to comprehend the Arabic language spoken in Tunis.

East

And it came to pass, as they journeyed from the east, that they found a plain in the land of Shinar; and they dwelt there. Gen. 11:2.

Madnekha in Aramaic means "the rising of the sun" or "east." The sun rises from the east; therefore, *madnekha,* metaphorically, also means light. In the Near East, the term "light" likewise means "truth." According to John's gospel, Jesus of Nazareth said, "I am the light of the world," meaning Jesus' teaching is truth. God is also referred to as Light. The sun, too, is symbolic of God because it pours out three attributes—light, heat, and color.

On the other hand, *maarba* derives from *erab*, meaning "sun setting," "darkness," or "west." In biblical days, people used the word "east" referring to going in the right direction toward light, truth, and good guidance, and the word "west" was often used to symbolize darkness, going astray, and moving away from the light.

"They journeyed from the east," symbolically means they strayed from the true path; that is, they forsook the ways of God. This is the reason people were confused and continued to wander aimlessly from place to place. When they strayed from the true path, they were deceived by the material world on which they relied for guidance and security. When people lose a true path, they wander after the imagination of their own hearts and confront problems and difficulties that they fail to solve or overcome.

Plural of Respect or Deliberation

Go to, let us go down, and there confound their language, that they may not understand one another's speech. Gen. 11:7.

Emperors, kings, princes, dignitaries, and high ecclesiastical authorities use the plural pronoun of respect, especially after making decisions. The "we" and "us" is noted as the plural of respect and deliberation. Naturally, when the writer has God speaking of himself and after a deliberation, "let us go down," the plural form must be used. The authors of holy Scripture believed in one God only, the God of heaven and earth.

"Hear, O Israel: the Lord our God is one Lord."[2] The Israelites

---

[2]Dt. 6:4, Mk. 12:29.

were admonished against having another god besides the Lord their God. The whole system of Israel's faith is based on the unity of God—one God. Near Eastern Semitic followers of Jesus believe in one God with three attributes instead of three persons.[3]

---

[3]See also the comments on Gen. 1:26, "Humankind," pp. 17-20, especially "God is one."

CHAPTER 12

Abraham Becoming a Blessing

And I will make of thee a great nation, and I will bless thee, and make thy name great; and thou shalt be a blessing; And I will bless them that bless thee, and curse him that curseth thee: and in thee shall all families of the earth be blessed. Gen. 12:2-3.

According to the biblical narrative, the departure of Abraham from his land, Ur of Chaldea, was preordained by God. Abraham was to have a major role in the divine plan, bringing a great blessing to the entire human family. Salvation and enlightenment would be bestowed on all the families of the earth.

The divine promise was made before Abraham departed from his native land and kindred. Abraham's reward for participating in the spiritual role for humanity was that he would become a great nation. He was called the blessed of the Lord God.[1]

The biblical text clearly reveals that God's design was a universal reign or kingdom and that Abraham and the nation Israel were simply agents in this plan. Before Abraham left his people, all the various tribes and nations were straying from the way of God, including many close kinsmen of Abraham. Therefore, God's purpose was for all the people of the world. Abraham's simple and uncomplicated faith was to embrace all races and nations of the earth. The Torah that was to be given to his descendants was destined to become a light to Israel and the Gentile world.

His descendants, who would become known as Israel, had a divine mission which was spiritual, not political. For many years the descendants of Abraham were under the divine guidance of God. All of this was leading to the coming of the messianic kingdom that would evince God's rule. The dominion of this kingdom was to be

---

[1]Gen. 14:19.

from sea to sea, and from the River Euphrates to the ends of the earth. All the nations of the world would participate in this godly and humane sovereignty.

The phrase, "And I will bless them that bless thee, and curse him that curseth thee," was a declaration of divine protection. This is the language that Abraham understood. In the ancient Near East, placing curses on people was common, especially on those who would wish to curse and hurt you. When Abraham heard this message in his dream, he knew God would protect him from anyone who might attempt to harm him.

Mamre

And Abram passed through the land unto the place of Sichem, unto the plain of Moreh. And the Canaanite was then in the land. Gen. 12:6.

The Eastern Aramaic Peshitta text reads *"Mamre"* instead of "Moreh." *"Mamre"* means a "dwelling place." It can also mean a temporary settlement like a *dera* where nomad people encamp for a long period of time but not permanently.

"Moreh" in the King James text of the verse above is a corrupt form for *Mamre* The error might have been caused during the transcription of the story from one Semitic alphabet into another, which often happens.

Mamre is near Hebron. Abraham traveled between Shechem in the north country and Hebron in the south, feeding his large flocks and seeking new wells and grazing rights from the native people.

Abraham, A Petty Ruler

The princes also of Pharaoh saw her, and commended her before Pharaoh: and the woman was taken into Pharaoh's house. Gen. 12:15.

In the Near East, an emir, or the head of a large tribe, was considered a petty ruler or a minor king; therefore, when he was traveling, especially with his entire tribe, kings, princes, and other petty rulers of various territories would show respect for his presence and would also honor him.

When Abraham arrived in Egypt, he had to pay his respects to Pharaoh and his princes. Had Abraham been all alone, he probably would not have been noticed in such a great country as Egypt, even though Abraham was a highly honored emir, the head of a large and prosperous tribe.

Both Abraham and his wife, Sarah, called on the Egyptian ruler, who welcomed them and probably invited them to live in one of his many palaces.

Beauty is Dangerous

The princes also of Pharaoh saw her, and commended her before Pharaoh: and the woman was taken into Pharaoh's house. And he entreated Abram well for her sake: and he had sheep, and oxen, and he asses, and menservants, and maidservants, and she asses, and camels. And the Lord plagued Pharaoh and his house with great plagues, because Sarai, Abram's wife. Gen. 12:15-17.

In ancient Near Eastern countries, and until the early 1900s, a man with a beautiful wife was not safe. The beauty of his wife could cost him his life. It often happened that the husband was killed and his wife was taken away by kings, princes, or high government officials, just as in the case of Bathsheba and David.[2]

Abraham was from Chaldea. Chaldean women were noted for being fair and beautiful, especially when compared with the dark-skinned Arab and Egyptian women. Also, Abraham was a stranger in Egypt and, as a Near Easterner, he had seen and heard that many men

---

[2]2 Sam. 1:15.

had lost their lives on account of their beautiful wives. He knew that his life would be in danger if Pharaoh should desire to have his wife, Sarah.

Therefore, the only alternative was to instruct his wife to pose as his sister. (Of course, in reality, Sarah was Abraham's half sister.[3]) Abraham had to do this, not for the sake of money and favors, as it might appear from reading the text, but to save his life and the lives of those who were with him. The whole tribe was in danger of perishing with famine. Putting it in modern language, Abraham was between the devil and the deep, blue sea. Evidently what Abraham had surmised began to happen. When Pharaoh's courtiers saw her, they went and praised her to Pharaoh; Sarah was then taken into Pharaoh's palace.

It is quite probable that Pharaoh attempted to discover why an affliction of plagues came on him and his household. He might have questioned Sarah, and she revealed to him the entire matter. Immediately Pharaoh sent for Abraham and questioned and rebuked him. Then he returned Sarah to Abraham, and they had to depart from the land of Egypt. It seems that the Egyptians had a moral code and were afraid of punishment for wrongdoing.

Isaac did the same thing when he went to Philistia because of a severe famine. His wife, Rebekah, was an Assyrian, and she also was fair and beautiful in appearance. Isaac instructed her not to tell the people that she was his wife but to say that she was his sister. Then, when Abimeleck, king of the Philistines, discovered that Rebekah was Isaac's wife, he immediately issued an order saying that anyone who molested her would be put to death. He then rebuked Isaac for having deceived him.[4]

---

[3]Gen. 20:12.
[4]Gen. 26:1, 6-11.

CHAPTER 13

Sodom

And Lot lifted up his eyes, and beheld all the plain of Jordan, that it was well watered every where, before the Lord destroyed Sodom and Gomorrah, even as the garden of the Lord, like the land of Egypt, as thou comest unto Zoar. Gen. 13:10.

The exact location of Sodom and Gomorrah (Aramaic: *Amorah*) is not known. It must have been either north or south of the Salt Sea, also known as the Dead Sea. These two cities must have been visible from Bethel. Some authorities maintain that the location of these cities might have been the marshy place near Mount Sodom.

Modern *Amoriah* is at the northwest corner of the Salt Sea. It might be the ancient Amorah. The region that Lot chose was a rich and extremely fertile land.

CHAPTER 14

Pitch Pits

And the vale of Siddim was full of slime pits; and the kings of Sodom and Gomorrah fled, and fell there; and they that remained fled to the mountain. Gen. 14:10.

The Aramaic word *qeera* means "pitch" or "asphalt." The valley of Siddim was full of bitumen pits. Pitch and other minerals are plentiful around the Salt Sea. Some biblical authorities maintain that the brimstone and fire was caused by the combustion of inflammable material. However that may have been, Lot was warned by the messengers in his dream that the place would become a disaster and that he would have to leave the region immediately.[1]

During the battle, the chariots were unable to operate in the hot plains of Jericho. Pitch melts during the hot hours of the day. The kings of Sodom and Amorah fell there, and those who survived fled to the mountain areas to hide.

Pitch is found in abundance in Mesopotamia and other parts of the Near East. It was the discovery of pitch in Assyria that helped the English geologists to find the rich oil fields in Iraq. Noah was instructed by God to cover the ark with pitch.[2]

Abraham, the Hebrew

And there came one that had escaped, and told Abram the Hebrew; for he dwelt in the plain of Mamre the Amorite, brother of Eshcol, and brother of Aner: and these were confederate with Abram. Gen. 14:13.

---

[1]Gen. 19:12-13.
[2]Gen. 6:14.

The term "Hebrew," *Ebrayah,* comes from the Aramaic root word *abar,* "to cross over," that is to say, the people across the river Euphrates. When Abraham and Lot, his nephew, left Haran and crossed the Euphrates on their way to Palestine, some of Abraham's tribal kinsmen chose to remain in Haran. This is the reason that those who crossed with Abraham were called *Ebrayeh,* "Hebrews." This name was given to them so that they could be distinguished from the other members of the clan who did not cross the river. In other words, the tribe that left with Abraham from Ur of Chaldea split in two as usually was the custom of the tribes of the Near East. A few years later, Lot's tribe split from Abraham and went into the region of Sodom and Gomorrah or the valley of Jericho. In Aramaic, people often say, "these are our people across the river" or "the people on the other side of the river."[3]

The Aramaic word *ebra* means "a crossing or landing place," such as the crossing place at Jordan. In the New Testament, Western translators confused this word with the Aramaic term *abar,* "to cross over," in the incident when the disciples were going by boat from the crossing place at Tiberias to the port of Capernaum. They did not cross the sea of Galilee to the Syrian side on this occasion.[4]

Abraham's Army

And when Abram heard that his brother was taken captive, he armed his trained servants, born in his own house, three hundred and eighteen, and pursued them unto Dan. Gen. 14:14.

---

[3]In scholarly opinion there exist three different interpretations on the origin and meaning of this term "Hebrew." One idea suggests that it derives from Eber, the grandson of Noah (Gen. 10:24, 11:14); another is the notion that we espouse; the third alludes to Abraham's religious nonconformity. For a more detailed discussion see Nahum M. Sarna, The JPS Torah commentary, GENESIS, "Excursus 4, Abraham the Hebrew," pp. 377-378.

[4]Mt. 14:22, Mk. 6:45, Jn. 6:16-17.

Abraham was the emir or chief of a very large tribe. The author of the book of Genesis gives us the impression that Abraham was only the head of a family. The reason for this is that in the Near East a tribe was known by the name of its emir or chief. Tribes in Arabia and other regions of the Near and Middle East are known by the name of their chiefs and their families.

Abraham had many men in his tribe. Some of them were tending sheep, others were herdsmen, and still others were performing the main duties of tribal needs. All the men who worked for Abraham and served as his soldiers had their own sheep and cattle. Abraham took with him 318 trained warriors, and as he trusted in God, this small force was sufficient to defeat his enemies.

The term "servants" does not mean "slaves." Again, in the Near East, members of the tribe when addressing their chief called him "our lord" and spoke of themselves as servants. It is believed that tribal life was one of the most ancient forms of democracy ever devised by man for that time. The chief of the tribe is considered as a father, and he regards all the members of his tribe as his children.

Bread and Wine

And Melchizedek king of Salem brought forth bread and wine: and he was the priest of the most high God. And he blessed him, and said, Blessed be Abram of the most high God, possessor of heaven and earth.
Gen. 14:18-19.

Melchizedek means "king of righteousness." It also suggests "the rightful king." Bread and wine symbolized friendship and loyalty. Bread is a life sustaining substance, and wine generally makes people's hearts merry.

Whenever a king, prince, or nobleman entered a town, he was greeted by the ruler, officials, and noblemen with bread and salt and other articles of food. In those ancient days, wine was probably used because of the lack of water. Until the early 1900s, in many regions of the Near and Middle East, salt and animals were offered to visiting royalty, government officials, and noblemen as tokens of welcome.

In those ancient countries, restaurants or eating places were rare. Travelers usually reached the town thirsty and hungry and, at times, almost starving. This very old custom is evident throughout Scripture and is still practiced regionally.

Being a petty ruler and chief of a very large and powerful tribe, Abraham caused Melchizedek, king of Salem (Jerusalem), to greet him with bread and wine. Abraham and his men were returning from battle victoriously, but they were hungry and thirsty. Such gifts on these occasions inspired friendship and confidence between the two rulers. Words and praises are soon forgotten, but gifts of welcome and good deeds are always remembered.

Melchizedek was a righteous priest and king, and Abraham also was the spiritual and political leader of his people. This is why Melchizedek said to him: "Blessed be Abraham of the most high God."

An example of failure to observe this custom is found in the book of Deuteronomy. The twelve tribes of Israel were traveling in the desert, making their way to the promised land. When they came to the border of the Ammonites and Moabites, these people did not greet them with bread and wine nor with water; therefore, the Israelites never forgot it.[5]

Another narrative is recorded about King David, but this time the ancient custom was practiced. The narrator informs the reader that when David was fleeing from his son, Absalom, Ziba brought him loaves of bread, raisins, summer fruits, and wine loaded on donkeys.[6]

Most High God

And blessed be the most high God, which hath delivered thine enemies

---

[5]Dt. 23:3-4.
[6]2 Sam. 16:1-2.

into thy hand. And he gave him tithes of all. Gen. 14:20.

Alaha Marayma means "Most High God" or "Exalted God." *Marayma* also means "dwelling in the highest," the God whose abode is in heaven. The dwelling place of other gods was on earth. Helpless statues and images of gods and goddesses were crowded in dark and dim temples and shrines.

During this time most people in those regions knew that there was a High God—that is, a greater God than the local deities they served. This concept of a Great Spirit was prevalent among all peoples and even among the native American tribes.

It is most probable that Melchizedek was a member of one of the Semitic tribes who had migrated early into the land of Canaan. Abraham had recognized him as a high priest of a true religion. Semites gained prominence wherever they went. The descendants of Abraham, Lot, Ishmael, Esau, and Jacob became kings and princes over other races. Melchizedek might have been a descendant of one of the Babylonian (Chaldean) high priests and a distant kin of Abraham.

Shalem or Salem, like Shiloh, was a place of worship and a meeting place where people made peace with God and settled their differences with one another. In Near Eastern Christian communities, priests and high priests used to act as judges and arbiters in all legal matters.

An Oath

And Abram said to the king of Salem, I have lifted up mine hand unto the Lord, the most high God, the possessor of heaven and earth. Gen.14:22.

"I have lifted up mine hand" is a Near Eastern saying that means, "I have sworn before God." Semites, when taking an oath, lifted their hands toward heaven and invoked the name of God, whom they made a witness to their oath: ". . .as a faithful witness in heaven."[7]

When treaties and agreements were made in the name of God, they were generally respected and kept even by future generations.[8] Other treaties and covenants were easily broken and repudiated, just as they are broken in our days.[9]

---

[7]Ps. 89:37, 1 Sam. 12:5.

[8]Jos. 9:18.

[9]Interestingly, to this day, Muslims and some of the Near Eastern Christians keep their sworn pledges and agreements. They lend money to each other on the strength of their oaths.

CHAPTER 15

Large Numbers

And he brought him forth abroad, and said, Look now toward heaven, and tell the stars, if thou be able to number them: and he said unto him, So shall thy seed be. Gen. 15:5.

In those days, large numbers, such as a hundred thousand, a million, and a billion were unknown. Even the figure one thousand was only known to some educated people. Simple folk, who used their fingers when counting, could not count beyond one hundred. The stars in heaven and the grains of sand on the seashore were understood as describing an extremely large number such as a million or a billion.

The term "seed" has several meanings: "offspring, descendants, teaching." The reference here is more to the faith of Abraham—that is, his teaching—than to just his blood descendants. Much later in the history of the Near East, many nations and people would embrace the religion of Abraham; therefore, he became their spiritual father and founder of their religion.

In biblical days, people who changed their religion also changed their race. Ruth was a Moabite, but when she accepted the God of Israel, she became a daughter of Abraham.

When Near Eastern Christians speak of Abraham, they refer to him as "Father Abraham." He became the father of many believers.[1] It was Abraham's faith that was counted as righteousness.[2]

Today, the spiritual descendants of Abraham are more than all the rest of the people in the world. Jews, Christians, and Muslims all believe in the God of Abraham and are his spiritual descendants.

---

[1]Gen. 17:4.
[2]Gen. 15:6.

Four Centuries

But in the fourth generation they shall come hither again: for the iniquity of the Amorites is not yet full. Gen. 15:16.

The Aramaic word *dareh* means "centuries." The Eastern Aramaic text reads, "four centuries," not "four generations." The Israelites were in Egypt about 430 years.[3] Four generations would be less than a hundred years. The Aramaic words for centuries, generations, and for conflict or struggle are written alike but pronounced differently. Therefore, such an error is almost unavoidable.[4]

In the New Testament this same error occurs in Acts 7:6. This misunderstanding is found in all Western versions of the Bible, including the Hebrew Masoretic text.

---

[3]Ex. 12:41.
[4]See Judges 11:26.

CHAPTER 16

Sarah's Handmaiden Hagar

Now Sarai, Abram's wife, bare him no children: and she had an handmaid, an Egyptian, whose name was Hagar. And Sarai said unto Abram, Behold now, the Lord hath restrained me from bearing: I pray thee, go in unto my maid; it may be that I may obtain children by her. And Abram hearkened to the voice of Sarai. And Sarai, Abram's wife took Hagar her maid the Egyptian, after Abram had dwelt ten years in the land of Canaan, and gave her to her husband Abram to be his wife. Gen. 16:1-3.

Semitic people have always practiced polygamy. Kings, princes, and noblemen had many wives and concubines. Abraham was an emir and entitled to have as many wives and servants as he needed.

Abraham had purchased Hagar for his wife, Sarah, who was also his half sister. At this time, Abraham was becoming older and was afraid that he would die childless and Eliezar, his servant, would inherit everything. But he kept remembering God's assurances that he would have an heir of his own, though not necessarily from Sarah.

Sarah had been barren for a long time and was also aging. Seeing that she would have no child of her own, Sarah persuaded Abraham to take Hagar, the Egyptian maidservant, and sleep with her. They needed an heir who would take care of them and their tribe. According to the biblical narrative, God blessed Ishmael and assured Abraham that twelve princes would come from this son.[1] Evidently, God was pleased with the matter.

The reader must keep in mind that this situation occurred about 2000 BCE. At that time, Semites were neither Jewish, Christian, or Muslim. Moses, the lawgiver, was born 400 years later. No law of God was broken when Abraham took Hagar to have an offspring. He was under no code of law, religious or otherwise, that forbade such

---

[1]Gen. 17:20.

an arrangement, nor was it a disgrace to do so. It was in accord with Near Eastern customs.

Ishmael

And he will be a wild man; his hand will be against every man, and every man's hand against him: and he shall dwell in the presence of all his brethren. Gen. 16:12.

Ishmael and his Egyptian mother were driven away by Sarah from the good land that God had promised to Abraham and his posterity. Now the Ishmaelites had to dwell in semiarid lands and deserts where water was scanty and grazing poor. As a nomad people, the descendants of Ishmael had to wander from one place to another seeking water and grass, and like the nomads of today, they would have to fight for their existence.

While roaming, the tribe transgressed the rights of other tribes and fought against them. Desert people are great fighters. Prior to the advent of Islam, many of the desert tribes had to raid and plunder one another so that they could make a living. These raiders were in turn raided and plundered by other tribes. The descendants of Ishmael were found all over the desert, and at times they invaded the land of their kindred tribes.[2]

The Well of the Living God

Wherefore the well was called Beerlahairoi: behold, it is between Kadesh and Bered. Gen. 16:14.

The Eastern Aramaic text reads: *baera-d-haya-hizani,* "the well of the living one who saw me." The Aramaic word *hizani* also means,

---

[2]Gen. 25:18.

"has seen my affliction," or "has taken care of me."[3] During this early period, the Hebrew tribe spoke the Aramaic language of their forefathers that they had learned in Padan-Aram, Mesopotamia, and Ur of Chaldea.

Hagar was lost in the vast desert and had given up hope of finding water to save herself and her unborn child. But the living God, the God of Abraham, had compassion on her. In a vision, God sent his messenger to direct her and assure her that the Lord's mercies were upon her and the unborn son, whose name was to be Ishmael. Ishmael means "God has heard me." *Shama* means "to hear" and *El*, "God."

---

[3]See Gen. 16:7-16, especially verse 13 in the Eastern Aramaic Peshitta text, Lamsa translation.

CHAPTER 17

El–Shaddai

And when Abram was ninety years old and nine, the Lord appeared to Abram, and said unto him, I am the Almighty God; walk before me, and be thou perfect. Gen. 17:1.

El-Shaddai is another name of the Hebrew Deity. It is usually translated as "Almighty." In Aramaic it signifies might and strength.[1] *El* means "God" and *Shaddai* connotes "power." The Arabic is *Shadidon.*

At this time, the Hebrews had a clearer concept of religion and God than other tribal peoples. They believed that God had created the heavens and the earth and everything in them. They believed that their God sent rain on the earth and caused grass to grow and trees to yield fruit. They knew that the Gentile gods and goddesses were nothing but helpless images and stone idols that could not even remove a fly from their faces.

Therefore, the Hebrew God was known as the God of power, might, and strength. They considered their God as the God of gods, the Author of life, and Provider of all human needs. The name *El-Shaddai* was coined by the Hebrews as a contrast between their God and the helpless gods of the Gentile tribes and nations that had ears but could not hear and eyes but could not see. *El-Shaddai* was all seeing and all knowing.[2]

---

[1]Gen. 49:25.

[2]For a detailed discussion on *El-Shaddai* see Errico, Rocco A., *Mysteries of Creation: The Genesis Story*, "El Shaddai," p. 64.

The Nickname Abram

Neither shall thy name any more be called Abram, but thy name shall be Abraham; for a father of many nations have I made thee. Gen. 17:5.

Abram means "high or exalted father," which was a nickname. In the Near East, men and women are known by their first names. The family name is used in deeds and documents only. Also, if there are two persons or more with the same name, the name of the father is used—for example, Jacob, son of Isaac, or Isaac, the father of Jacob.

Customarily, young men are called by their nicknames. Even young princes and noblemen are called by their nicknames until they become of age and occupy high positions in life, at which time they are no longer so addressed.

Abram now was the titular head of a large tribe, and he was to become the father of many people who were to believe in the one God. He would also become known as the father of the faithful. The Lord addressed him as Abraham because the members of the tribe were no longer to call him Abram. This is also true of Sarai. She was no longer to be addressed by her nickname Sarai, "princess," but Sarah, "princess of God."[3]

Seed—Teaching

And I will establish my covenant between me and thee and thy seed after thee in their generations for an everlasting covenant, to be a God unto thee, and to thy seed after thee. Gen. 17:7.

"Seed" in Aramaic not only means descendants and offspring but also is a metaphoric term for "teaching." In the prayer books of the Church of the East, people often read, "The seed that the apostles sowed throughout the world," meaning, "The gospel (teaching) of Christ that had been published all over the world."

---

[3]Gen. 17:15.

In the New Testament and according to the gospels, Jesus also likened his teaching on the kingdom of God to seed. In Aramaic his parable is called "The parable of the seed" and not "the parable of the sower." The reason for this is that the precious grain or seed has the capacity to multiply itself abundantly when planted. This is also true of the printed or spoken word. A word can be published from one corner of the earth to the other. One could take, for example, the words that once came from the lips of Jesus and his disciples 2,000 years ago but are now published in more than 1,000 languages and dialects.

In this passage, the term "seed of Abraham" not only refers to his progeny or offspring but also to the Spirit, because the promise was made not simply to all of his descendants but also to the heirs of his faith. Therefore, Abraham came to be called the father of the faithful.[4] The descendants of Ishmael and Esau were also the offspring of Abraham but not the heirs of the promise.

According to Scripture, the family of King David, because of his faithfulness to God, became an heir to God's promises, or an heir of the divine promise that was made to Abraham. As we have said, all the children of Israel are offspring of Abraham, but not all of his descendants were heirs to the promise.

In the realm of the Spirit, all the children of Abraham who believed in his religion and walked in God's way were children of the promise and heirs of Abraham. This is also true for the Gentiles who believe in the faith of Abraham. God's promise to Abraham is a blessing to all peoples of the world.

Circumcision

And ye shall circumcise the flesh of your foreskin; and it shall be a token of the covenant betwixt me and you. Gen. 17:11.

The primary objective of circumcision was the sealing of the

---

[4]Rom. 4:11.

covenant that God made with Abraham and his descendants. In the Near East, covenants or agreements were sealed with human blood. At times, sheep were slaughtered, roasted, and eaten when celebrating an agreement.

There were probably other reasons beyond the ancient custom of sealing a covenant with blood. Interestingly, Abraham and his people were not circumcised when they were in Ur of Chaldea and in Haran. This was probably due to the fact that there was abundant water and the people bathed themselves frequently. But in the land of Canaan there was a scarcity of water and the people rarely bathed.

Because bathing was unknown in desert lands where water was scarce, people often were prone to skin disorders. Without enough water and proper bathing, the men suffered at times with infections of the foreskin. The term "flesh" is a euphemistic term referring to the male genitalia. In those ancient days, where passports were unknown, tribal people were identified by the marks on their bodies and by the dialect or language that they spoke. So this, also, was a way of identification. Circumcision was employed by the Hebrew people who were with and under Abraham. Regardless of these other reasons, the biblical narrator emphasizes circumcision as part of the covenant with God.

Bless Him

And I will bless her, and give thee a son also of her: yea, I will bless her, and she shall be a mother of nations; kings of people shall be of her. Gen. 17:16.

The Aramaic text reads: "And I will bless her, and also I will give you a son by her; yea, I will bless him and make nations of him; and the kings of the people shall come from him."[5] The last part of the verse reads, "I will bless him," instead of, "her." The Aramaic masculine pronoun *ebarkeewhi* has been confused with the feminine

---

[5]Gen. 17:16, Eastern Aramaic Peshitta text, Lamsa translation.

114

pronoun *ebarkeeh*. The basic difference between the masculine and feminine pronouns is done by placing a square dot over the Aramaic letter *heh*, *"h,"* for the feminine gender. The reference here is to Isaac, who was to be the father of many nations, and the kings of these people were to be from his descendants.

Isaac was the ancestor not only of the twelve tribes of Israel but also of the powerful tribes of the children of his first-born, Esau (or Edom). God blessed both Sarah and her offspring, Isaac, but the second blessing in this verse was bestowed on Isaac, who was to become the father of many nations.[6] In the Near East, the blessings are generally invoked on the husband. The wife is blessed through him.

Sarah Ninety Years Old

Then Abraham fell upon his face, and laughed, and said in his heart, Shall a child be born unto him that is an hundred years old? And shall Sarah, that is ninety years old, bear? Gen. 17:17.

This episode may have happened years later. For in Genesis 20:1-2, we read that when Abraham went to the south country and dwelt between Kadesh and Shur and sojourned in Gerar, Abimeleck, the king of Gerar, sent for and took Sarah. Abraham had told her not to say that she was his wife but to say she was his sister, fearing that Abimeleck would slay him and take Sarah, as was often done in the Near East when a man had a beautiful wife.

Kings and princes generally took young women and virgins, but they respected elderly women, especially women who were ninety years of age. Therefore, had Sarah been ninety years old when Abraham was traveling in Gerar, he would not have been afraid of Abimeleck slaying him on account of his wife.

Sarah must have been attractive enough in her young years to win the favor of the king of Gerar, who had many wives and could

---

[6]See Gen. 17:19.

marry as many women as he pleased. The reader must take into consideration that many of these stories were handed down orally. Others were written, but when they were compiled, they were not always placed in proper time sequence.

God had already promised Abraham that Sarah would bear a child the next year.[7] Therefore, Sarah must have been with child before Abraham went to Gerar. One must also consider that in those days, a woman of eighty or ninety years of age retained her beauty, strength, and charm. Miriam, the sister of Moses, was about eighty-seven when she sang and danced in the Israelite camp.[8]

God Went Up

And he left off talking with him, and God went up from Abraham. Gen. 17:22.

The Aramaic word *ittreem,* "lifted up" or "went up," means, "went away" or "departed."[9] People in those days believed that God's abode was in the skies or heaven and that God descended to earth when communing with people. They did not have the knowledge that God was everywhere. When the people prayed, they implored God to come down and deliver them. The narrator even has God saying: "Let us go down and there confound their language."[10]

This concept concerning God's heavenly habitation prevailed for many centuries. Later the belief was revised by the Hebrew prophets and confirmed, according to John's gospel, by Jesus of Nazareth who taught that God is Spirit and that the divine presence is everywhere.[11]

---

[7]Gen. 18:10.
[8]Ex. 15:20.
[9]Gen. 18:33.
[10]Gen. 11:7.
[11]Jn. 4:24.

CHAPTER 18

Divine Guests

And the Lord appeared unto him in the plains of Mamre: and he sat in the tent door in the heat of the day; And he lifted up his eyes and looked and lo, three men stood by him: and when he saw them, he ran to meet them from the tent door, and bowed himself toward the ground. Gen. 18:1-2.

Near Easterners rest during the hot hours of the day. In Egypt, Arabia, and other countries where the climate is warm, work is suspended at noon. People rest and sleep until the day begins to cool.

Chiefs of the tribes, such as Abraham, as well as the rich and the noble, sleep on the shady side of their tents or at their openings to escape the heat and also to enjoy the breeze.

While Abraham was sleeping, in his vision (dream) he lifted up his eyes and looked, and all of a sudden he saw three noblemen standing a little distance from him. He thought that they were the chiefs of some of the neighboring tribes who had come to visit him. This unannounced visitation was a common practice among tribal, desert emirs or chiefs.

So Abraham ran to greet them and offered them typical Eastern hospitality, which is usually extended by one tribal head to another. He asked the chief lord that if he had found mercy in his sight to not pass by but remain so he could bring a little water, wash their feet, and they could rest under the shade of the tree. Abraham referred to himself as their servant. He also would serve them a meal. After urging them to remain, as a Near Eastern Semite host would do to his guests, they accepted his hospitality.

Abraham and Sarah hastened to make preparations to entertain the three guests, not knowing who they were. After washing their feet, and according to custom, they set a table before them. (They spread a large cloth or rug on the ground with trays of food.) The Lord and the two messengers (angels) who accompanied him ate meat, bread,

117

and other food that Sarah had carefully prepared. Then, after announcing that Sarah would bear a child, they departed. And as is the custom, Abraham accompanied them for a short distance, perhaps a mile or two; then the Lord revealed to him the coming catastrophe of Sodom and Gomorrah. The Lord told Abraham that he was going to see if the reports that came from there were true or not.[1]

Chapter 19: 27-28 reads: "And Abraham rose up early in the morning and went to the place where he had stood before the Lord. . . . and lo, the smoke of the country went up like the smoke of a furnace." Both Abraham and Lot were informed in their visions about the impending disaster that was to fall upon Sodom and Gomorrah.

God is Spirit and Truth. God has no feet to be washed, nor does God eat and drink. But in a vision or dream, God appears to people as one of them. This is the reason that the Lord God acts as a human, a man going to see if what he heard about Sodom and Gomorrah were true. As a man, he had to check out the place to know if the things the people were doing were evil. This was Abraham's vision, so he sees and communes with God as if God were a human being.

Abraham was a man of God and had seen many visions in his lifetime. According to the narrator, Abraham was always guided by God throughout all of his years living in Canaan. His spirituality was so strong that he could commune with God as one would commune with another person. His dreams continually guided him.

The Washing of Feet

Let a little water, I pray you, be fetched, and wash your feet, and rest yourselves under the tree. Gen. 18:4.

Washing the feet of the newly arrived guests and giving them water to drink and food to eat is a very old custom. In biblical lands, where the chief occupation was raising sheep and cattle, roads were

---

[1]See Gen. 18:21.

bad and, in some areas, dusty and muddy. Many people wore sandals, while some walked barefoot. When travelers arrived in sheep camps or towns, the host saw to it that their feet were washed. Then he seated them on quilts and *namdas* (bedding made of lambs' wool), rugs, and other bed clothes in which both the family and the guests slept during the night. The guests' feet were washed to keep the bed clothes clean.

Years later, it became an established custom or ritual and a sign of hospitality. In the gospel narrative, Simon the Pharisee refused to wash Jesus' feet because his teaching was questioned by the temple authorities and some synagogue leaders. But a woman who was a sinner washed Jesus' feet with her tears.[2] And, according to the gospel of John, Jesus himself washed the feet of his disciples.[3]

Cream

And he took butter, and milk, and the calf which he had dressed, and set it before them; and he stood by them under the tree, and they did eat. Gen. 18:8.

The Aramaic word *haewtha* in this verse means "cream." Pastoral and tribal people always placed cream before their honored guests. At times, cream is saved just for this purpose. The cream from the milk of sheep and goats is very delicious and is greatly coveted by the people. It would be embarrassing for a wealthy family not to have cream when a distinguished man is entertained. Butter is usually placed before common guests and workers.

Abraham entertained the Lord God, who came disguised as a tribal chief, with his two messengers (angels) in a vision. They ate and drank and had their discussions in a vision.

---

[2]Lk. 7:36-50.
[3]Jn. 13:4-10.

Pregnancy

And he said, I will certainly return unto thee according to the time of life; and lo, Sarah thy wife shall have a son. And Sarah heard it in the tent door, which was behind him. Gen. 18:10.

The Eastern Aramaic text reads: "And the Lord said, I will certainly return to you at this time next year, and lo, Sarah, your wife shall be with child, and shall have a son. And Sarah heard it in the tent door which was behind her.[4]

Once again a mistake in the pronoun appears in the King James version. It is the feminine pronoun that closes the tenth verse and not the masculine. God assures Abraham that he will have a son and that the heir will come directly from her.

Now in this vision, it is Sarah's turn to laugh. In another vision, Abraham laughed when God told him he would have a son from Sarah. This is one reason why Abraham named his son Isaac, "laughter." Nothing is impossible with God even when all hope seems to be gone and everything appears to be too late. God can still bring about a reversal of any situation.

Homage to Divine Guests

And the men rose up from thence, and looked toward Sodom: And Abraham went with them to bring them on the way. Gen. 18:16.

Near Eastern Semites generally welcome their notable guests and high government officials by meeting them on the way and escorting them to the town or, as in this narrative, to the encampment. Also, when the guests leave, the host accompanies them for a few miles to bring them out to the highway. People do this as a sign of great esteem and respect. This is even more true of the small villages and

---

[4]Gen. 18:10, Eastern Aramaic Peshitta text, Lamsa translation.

sheep camps where the roads, being narrow paths, are difficult to find.

Abraham, in his divine vision, accompanied the Lord and the two angels until he brought them to the highway and saw them off. Then he paid homage to God as he would do for any desert king or chief of a tribe. Early in the morning Abraham looked from the place where he had communed with the Lord in his dream and beheld that the cities of Sodom and Gomorrah (*Amorah*) were already burning.[5]

---

[5]Gen. 19:27-28.

CHAPTER 19

The Two Messengers in Sodom

*And there came two angels to Sodom at even: and Lot sat in the gate
of Sodom: and Lot seeing them rose up to meet them; and he bowed himself
with his face toward the ground. Gen. 19:1.*

The term angel in Aramaic has many meanings: ambassador,
messenger, preacher, a good man, holy man, a man of God, principal
elder, minister of a congregation. In the book of the Revelation, John
was asked to write to the angels of the seven churches in Asia Minor
(Turkey), that is, to the head ministers of the seven churches.[1] Angels,
malakheh, are also considered spirits.

According to this biblical episode, these are the same two
messengers who had appeared with the Lord to Abraham when he
was asleep at the door of his tent. The narrator connects them with
Abraham's vision. Now they also appear in a vision to Lot, Abraham's nephew. In his vision, Lot was seated at the gate of the city
when the two pious-looking strangers appeared. He immediately rose
up and invited them to come into his house as his guests.

In the Near East, when strangers were found at the gate, they
were invited into the homes and given food and lodging. Hotels and
special lodging places were unknown. Near Easterners often say:
"Today, he is my guest; tomorrow I will be his guest." Lot did what
any noble Arab chief would do.

NEAR EASTERNERS DECLINE INVITATIONS

"And he said, Behold now, my lord, turn in, I pray you, into your
servant's house, and tarry all night, and wash your feet, and ye shall
rise up early, and go on your ways. And they said, Nay; but we will

---

[1]Rev. 1:20.

abide in the street all night."[2] Nearly all Near Easterners will decline invitations to eat or to lodge until they are urged repeatedly to come into one's home. The host knows that the strangers do not mean it when they decline a cordial invitation. The visitors know they need food and lodging, but they must follow Near Eastern manners.

It is an ancient custom to decline until the host asks at least seven times. The angels of the Lord who appeared to Lot declined his hospitality, but they knew that he would insist that they come with him and spend the night in his home. The vision was so real that Lot was conversing with the angels (spirits) as though they were men.

THE CRIMES OF SODOM AND GOMORRAH

The inhabitants of Sodom and Gomorrah were so wicked and perverted that they would not even aid strangers who were at the gate. Oppression and violence were the crimes of these two cities. Sodom was a lewd and licentious city, where the men sought heinous vileness. In this narrative, the men of Sodom sought to rape Lot's guests. In his dream, Lot offered his virgin daughters, but they refused them and wanted the messengers of God. They would rather choose to disgrace his honorable guests. Raping them would shame them forever. Violence and mistreatment was their way of life.

The entire episode that depicts the men of Sodom desiring to rape God's ambassadors was a symbolic representation of the crimes of the inhabitants. It was a total disregard to strangers. They were so evil that they would even rape messengers of God. The narrator tells this heinous story because it was the best way of showing the consummate contempt and disrespect for human life in these wicked cities. Ezekiel, when indicting Jerusalem and also Samaria, names the sins of Sodom: "Behold, this is the iniquity of Sodom your proud sister: she and her daughters had abundant food and lived in tranquillity, but she did not help the poor and needy. And they were haughty and committed evil before me; therefore when I saw these things in

---

[2]Gen. 19:2, K. J. V.

them I overthrew them."[3] Sodom's townsfolk were corrupt in everything they represented. To put it another way, the narrator makes his case for the utter destruction of the cities, which were never to be rebuilt again. From the author's point of view, the inhabitants were getting what they deserved. Nevertheless, in the vision the angels struck the nefarious men with blindness, so they could not carry out their brutal scheme. As soon as Lot awakened from his dream, he understood the terrible consequences of living in Sodom.

Lot was warned by God's messengers to leave the doomed city and area at once. "And the men said to Lot, What are you doing in this place? Now, your sons-in-law, your sons, your daughters, and whatsoever you have in this city, take them out of this place; For we will destroy this place, because the cry of the oppressed has come before the Lord; and the Lord has sent us to destroy it."[4] The meaning and interpretation of the vision informed Lot that one day the townsmen might attack him. The reader has also learned, through Abraham's vision, that there were not even ten pious people who lived in the region. Lot, like Abraham, understood his vision.

THE STATUS OF WIVES

"Then Lot went out and spoke to his sons-in-law, who married his daughters, and said, Arise, get out of this place; for the Lord will destroy it. But his sons-in-law thought he was joking. And when the morning dawned, the angels urged Lot, saying, Arise, take your wife and your two daughters who are not given in marriage, lest you be engulfed in the sins of the city."[5]

In the Near East, the status of a married woman was different from a concubine. The additional phrase, "who married his daughters," was recorded by the author of Genesis so that he could reveal that Lot's daughters were given in marriage to his sons-in-law. Had

---

[3]Ezk. 16:49-50, Eastern Aramaic Peshitta text, Lamsa translation.
[4]Gen. 19: 12-13, Eastern Aramaic Peshitta text, Lamsa translation.
[5]Gen. 19:14-15, Eastern Aramaic Peshitta text, Lamsa translation.

they been concubines or slaves, their masters could not be called sons-in-law. For example, King Solomon had seven hundred wives whom he had married, and three hundred concubines who were presented to him as gifts and who had no status as wives. This was also true of Abraham and Hagar; the latter was not considered a full fledged wife. This is why Sarah could easily put her away.

Lot obeyed the voice of God and, directed by the angels, left the city in the early morning and fled to Zoar (Aramaic: "Little."), a small town in the mountains of Moab.

A great many episodes in the Bible are based on visions that men of God saw. The books of the prophets were based on their visions and revelations which, at times, they were told to write.[6]

Looking Behind

And it came to pass, when they had brought them forth abroad, that he said, Escape for thy life; look not behind thee, neither stay thou in all the plain; escape to the mountain, lest thou be consumed. Gen. 19:17.

"Do not look behind" is an idiom and can also mean, "Do not regret" or "forget the past." Lot had chosen the plain of Jordan, the well-watered land that was like a garden and like the fields of Zoan in Egypt, but the arid region west of Jordan was left to Abraham.[7]

Lot, although faithful to the voice of God, was somewhat reluctant to leave. Some of his daughters were married in Sodom and Gomorrah and had considerable properties in the land. It was not an easy matter to not think of the past in such a fertile valley where one harvest comes after another throughout the year. But Lot was warned by God to leave immediately so that he and his family could escape the impending disaster that was to befall the doomed region. On such an occasion every minute counts.

---

[6]See Hab. 2:2.
[7]Gen. 13:10.

Lot was also warned not to stay in the plain but to escape to the mountains. The whole region of the plain was to be destroyed with a powerful fire of chemicals and brimstone. Even an hour of delay would have caused Lot and his family to be engulfed by the great disaster. The entire region of the plain that contained pitch was to be ablaze.

Pillar of Salt

But his wife looked back from behind him, and she became a pillar of salt. Gen. 19:26.

"She became a pillar of salt" is a Semitic idiom, meaning "She had a stroke" or "she became paralyzed and died." In the Near East, when a man becomes paralyzed or suffers a stroke, people say: "He has turned into a rock or a stone."

In another biblical episode, when Abigail told her husband Nabal that she had given provisions to David and his men who were fleeing from King Saul, he became so enraged that he suffered a heart attack. Scripture records it as: ". . . and his wife had told him these things, that his heart died within him, and he became as a stone."[8] And yet, according to the next verse (38), Nabal died ten days after he had become stone. Had he literally become a stone, he could not have lived for ten days more. These idioms are still in use among Aramaic speaking people of the Near East.

Lot's wife had been reluctant to leave the pleasant gardens and orchards of Sodom. She had doubted her husband's vision and the divine warning to flee immediately. Her sons-in-law thought that Lot had lost his mind and that he was joking when he told them of the impending disaster, asking them to leave the city.[9] Evidently, Lot's wife also did not believe the cities would be destroyed.

---

[8] 1 Sam. 25:37, K. J. V.
[9] See Gen. 19:14.

Lot's wife did not heed the divine command and looked behind, and when she saw the city of lush orchards and gardens and everything that was dear to her heart on fire and the smoke rising to the high heavens, she suffered a stoke. She became hard like a block of salt or flint rock, which is also called salt. She died from the terrible shock of the sight she beheld. Interestingly, such blocks of slate rock are still to be found in Sodom.

The catastrophe and the loss of her daughters, sons-in-law, and other relatives were too much for a woman who had been accustomed to living in the luxuries of Sodom and who had no faith in the God of her husband. The lesson here is that Lot's wife became stricken and died because of her unfaithfulness and disregard of God's command.

No Kindred Left

And the firstborn said unto the younger, Our father is old and there is not a man in the earth to come in unto us after the manner of all the earth. Gen. 19:31.

The Aramaic term *araa* in this passage means, "land, region," not the earth. There were other tribal people throughout the region and the area of the Jordan, such as Hittites, Amorites, Syrians, and Canaanites. But all these people were corrupt and did not worship the Hebrew God. All the men and women who belonged to the families of Abraham and Lot had perished in Sodom and Gomorrah.

Lot's daughters were unwilling to marry men of other tribes who did not worship their God. Abraham and his tribe were on the other side of the River Jordan. During this early time, all Hebrew patriarchs were opposed to intermarriage with the natives of the region.[10] Lot's daughters wanted to preserve the continuity of their own family. Had they married other tribal men, Lot's name would have been obliterated and his posterity lost forever.

---

[10]Gen. 24:1-4.

Lot's Daughters

Come, let us make our father drink wine, and we will lie with him, that we may preserve seed of our father. And they made their father drink wine that night: and the first born went in, and lay with her father; and he perceived not when she lay down, nor when she arose. Gen. 19:32-33.

The Hebrews had a code of morals that was older than the Mosaic law and its ordinances. This code was handed down orally, just as the nomad tribes keep oral treaties and preserve moral laws that are handed down from one generation to another.

For example, they never married sisters, daughters, and other near kinsmen. Lot's case was dictated by emergency. Apparently, Lot's daughters had no one of their kindred to marry. They had just fled from Sodom, where their relatives and friends had perished in the earthquake. They thought that in order to preserve their lineage, they had to co-habit with their father.

They knew their father, being a pious man, would not consent to lie with them, so they made him drink wine until he was drunk. Lot had intercourse with both of his daughters without realizing with whom he slept. When a man is inflamed with wine, he does not always know what he is doing. "For wine is a mocker."[11]

There is another interpretation to this story concerning Lot's daughters. Biblical Hebrew scholars J. Cheryl Exum and J. William Whedbee believe that many biblical narratives are involved with comedy and tragedy. They inform us that the author of Genesis interrupts the flow of Isaac's short birth account with ethnic humor—that is, the story of Lot and his two daughters.[12]

These biblical commentators write: "Such use of an invented story about the questionable origins of one's hated relatives is a

---

[11]Prov. 20:1, 23:20-21.

[12]See Errico, Rocco A. *Let There Be Light: The Seven Keys,* "Comic and Humorous Elements in Scripture," for the story of Lot and his two daughters, pp. 122-123, Revised and Expanded, second edition, 1994.

stock-in-trade strategy of ethnic humour. In fact, according to Fyre, "the possibilities of incestuous combinations form one of the minor themes of comedy."[13]

[13]Yehuda T. Radday and Athalya Brenner, editors *On Humour and the Comic in the Hebrew Bible,* "Isaac, Samson, and Saul: Reflections on the Comic and Tragic Visions," pp. 124-125, J. Cheryl Exum and J. William Whedbee,

CHAPTER 20

Abimeleck Takes Sarah

But Abimelck had not come near her: and he said, Lord, wilt thou slay also a righteous nation? Gen. 20:4.

In biblical times, when monarchs or petty rulers took new wives, they did not have intimacy with them right away. They had to wait for a certain period of time. Women were examined, purified, and prepared to be acceptable to the ruler. Esther had to wait twelve months to undergo the treatment prescribed for women.[1]

Abimeleck took Sarah, believing that she was Abraham's sister. (She was a half sister and a wife.) Abraham, fearing for his life, had told Sarah not to say that she was his wife. When a man had a beautiful wife, his life was in danger. But when a man had a pretty sister, he was welcomed and given many gifts.

Evidently, it was during the time of Sarah's preparation and prescribed treatments that the Lord spoke to Abimeleck in a dream at night and warned him that Sarah was the wife of Abraham. The king hastily returned her to her husband, Abraham. Abimeleck had not approached her. In the same way, Sarah had also been taken by Pharaoh.[2]

Abraham, a Prophet

Now therefore restore the man his wife; for he is a prophet, and he shall pray for thee, and thou shalt live; and if thou restore her not, know thou that thou shalt surely die, thou, and all that are thine. Gen. 20:7.

---

[1]Esther 2:12.
[2]Gen. 12:15.

All patriarchs and pious men who communed with God in visions were addressed as prophets, seers, or men of God. A prophet is a spokesman for God and communicates with God.

Throughout the latter part of his life, Abraham was in constant union with God and remained faithful to the divine presence. This is the reason he was called the father of believers. Prophets were considered representatives of God and were revered more than priests. But Abraham left no writings, delivered no oracles, never acted as a counselor to kings, nor was he a teacher. In his day writing was in its infancy and difficult. All other prophets either left writings or a book, and they taught, gave counsel, and admonished their people. Nevertheless, Abraham was a chieftain and a prophet.

Muslims also call Abraham a prophet and his name is listed in the Koran as one of God's prophets. Abraham heard the voice of God for directions in his life and he always acted on it. He was constantly guided by God and fulfilled whatever God showed him to do; therefore, he was considered a man of God.

Abimeleck, a Righteous Man

And Abimeleck said unto Abraham, What sawest thou, that thou hast done this thing? And Abraham said, Because I thought, Surely the fear of God is not in this place and they will slay me for my wife's sake.
Gen. 20:10-11.

Many of the people in the land of Canaan revered and feared the Lord God of the Hebrews. These people also had an oral or written code that prohibited adultery. Abimeleck was seemingly a righteous man who respected his neighbor's wife. He had taken Sarah because of her beauty, thinking that she was Abraham's sister.

Nomad tribes practiced polygamy, but they respected one another's wives as their own sisters and mothers. A moral code of law must have existed in the Land of Canaan, Egypt, and Assyria prior to the Mosaic law. The laws of Khomarabi (Hammurabi, king of

Babylonia) were written before the days of Abraham. It is the first recorded moral code in human history.

When Abraham prayed, Abimeleck was healed. According to the story teller, the Lord forgave the king of Gerar because he was innocent and ignorant in the entire matter.

A Humiliating Reproach

And unto Sarah he said, Behold, I have given thy brother a thousand pieces of silver: behold, he is to thee a covering of the eyes, unto all that are with thee, and with all other: thus she was reproved. Gen. 20:16.

The Eastern Aramaic text reads: "And to Sarah he said, Behold, I have given a thousand pieces of silver to your brother; behold, it is given for you, because you have been humbled in the eyes of my people, and because of the other things for which I have reproved you."[3]

Sarah had posed as the sister of Abraham, and because of the stories she had told the people in the palace, she was humiliated. In the Near East, when a person is humbled or exposed, people who stand near the shamed person cover their faces on account of the reproach and deception.

Abimeleck paid Abraham one thousand pieces of silver so that he could absolve himself of any guilt in the matter, even though he had not touched her. He also had to make some kind of recompense because Sarah had been humiliated and bore a shame in the eyes of the people. She had become a reproach.

---

[3]Gen. 20:16, Eastern Aramaic Peshitta text, Lamsa translation.

CHAPTER 21

Hagar and Ishmael

And God said unto Abraham, Let it not be grievous in thy sight because of the lad, and because of thy bondwoman; in all that Sarah hath said unto thee, hearken unto her voice; for in Isaac shall thy seed be called. Gen. 21:12.

Bondwoman is another term for maidservant. Bondwomen had no status; therefore, they were not called wives. Some of them were slave women whom men had bought with money or taken captive. They could be dispossessed and put away at any time. Hagar, here, is addressed not as a wife but as a bondwoman—that is, a piece of property.

Seed in this verse means not only "posterity" but also the "teaching" or "faith" of Abraham that was to become a major religion in the world. Through this faith all the nations and peoples of the world were to be blessed. Messianic promises were to be fulfilled through the descendants of Isaac. Later, Esau was rejected and Jacob was chosen.

Ishmael was not rejected simply because his mother was an Egyptian. Ishmael had no fault in being born of a slave woman; God blessed him and made him a great nation. Many princes came forth from the lineage of Abraham and Hagar's son.

The covenant was made and confirmed with Isaac before his birth.[1] Ishmael is the ancestor of Muhammed, the prophet of Islam. Millions of men and women heard of the God of Abraham through Muhammed. The descendants of Ishmael are far more numerous than those of Jacob.[2]

---

[1] Gen. 17:21.
[2] Gen. 17:20, 21:13.

Weighty Burdens

And Abraham rose up early in the morning and took bread, and a bottle of water, and gave it unto Hagar, putting it on her shoulder and the child, and sent her away: and she departed, and wandered in the wilderness of Beer-sheba. Gen. 21:14.

Travelers in the Near and Middle East carried bread and water on a journey. Distances between towns were long. Bread and water could not be easily obtained while traveling. This still holds true for many regions of Arabia. In those ancient days water was carried in a sheep skin or goat skin.

Jesus and his disciples carried bread on their journeys and, at times, when their bread was exhausted, they went hungry.

When Joseph sent his brothers to the land of Canaan to bring their father, Jacob, to Egypt, he gave them provisions for their journey.[3]

In the Near East, it is not unusual to see a woman carrying a heavy burden with a child on top of it. Near Eastern women, during migrations, often carry burdens and place one of their children on them. Many mothers would hate to see their only child walking while they were carrying only a light load.

Hagar's burden consisted of ample provisions for the journey, probably a goat skin filled with water, and her son Ishmael. The latter is still referred to as a child, although he was about thirteen years old when Abraham circumcised him.[4] Since Hagar was a slave woman, Abraham wanted her to carry Ishmael, who was awakened in the early morning.

Ishmael was Abraham's son and, therefore, was spoiled. The sons of emirs and rulers seldom walked. They were carried by servants or rode on horses or donkeys.

---

[3]Gen. 45:21-23. See also Jos. 9:5.
[4]Gen. 17:25.

The Hidden Well Found

And God opened her eyes, and she saw a well of water; and she went and filled the bottle with water, and gave the lad drink. Gen. 21:19.

The well was always there, but Hagar couldn't find it. Her mind was confused and embittered toward her mistress, Sarah. After all, it was really Sarah who had expelled her and her only child. She was in a terrible predicament.

But when Hagar forgot her troubles and bitterness over Abraham's wife, she turned to God and prayed for help. After calling upon God, her mind cleared and her eyes were opened and she looked around and discovered the well.

When our spiritual vision becomes blurred, our eyes become blind and cannot see the answers to the dilemma. But when we turn to God for spiritual guidance, our eyes lose their blindness and see the right way, and the sources of help are made known.

Beer-Sheba

Wherefore he called that place Beer-sheba; because there they sware both of them. Gen. 21:31.

Beer-Sheba is an Aramaic compound noun that means "the seventh well." *Beer* means "well," *Sheba*, "seven."

Abraham gave Abimeleck seven ewe lambs as a witness that he had dug the seven wells. The wells were the property of Abraham (verses 29-30). The seven ewes were the reminder of the seven wells that belonged to Abraham.

Water was scanty in Arabia, and in that region, the shepherds fought over the wells. At times, princes and powerful chiefs ruthlessly confiscated wells.[5]

---

[5]Gen. 21:25, 26:15-18.

In Genesis 26:33, the name of the well is called *Shebah*, Hebrew for "oath." *Sabaa* in Aramaic means "plenty." Isaac found a prolific well of running water; therefore, the term was given a new meaning. Hebrew was not yet spoken at that time.

God of the Worlds

And Abraham planted a grove in Beer-sheba, and called there on the name of the Lord, the everlasting God. Gen. 21:33.

The Eastern Aramaic text reads: "And Abraham planted a grove in Beer-sheba and he called there on the name of the Lord God of the worlds."[6] The phrase in Aramaic reads: *Mariah Alaha dalmeh*. The Aramaic word for "everlasting" is *alam*.

In the previous verses, God had communed with Abimeleck, the ruler of Gerar, and warned him to return Sarah to her husband, Abraham.[7] Also, some years before, God revealed that the plague that befell the Pharaoh was because he had taken Sarah into his harem of wives. So God warned him that he must restore Sarah to Abraham.[8] Now Abraham, because of these episodes in his life, began to realize that his God was the God of all peoples.

At this time, Abraham felt he needed to plant a grove in Beer-sheba and invoke the name of the Lord God of the worlds, the living and everlasting God. Beer-sheba was a good place in which he could settle. He planted the grove not to worship the trees as the other tribal people did but to provide shelter from the sun. Also the trees would bear fruit for the people who were with him.

In the Near East, when one plants a grove of trees in a certain place, that individual becomes the recognized owner of that property. Abraham wanted a place that he could call his own.

---

[6]Errico translation.
[7]Gen. 20:7.
[8]Gen. 12:17.

CHAPTER 22

Abraham's Vision: The Offering of Isaac

And it came to pass after these things, that God did tempt Abraham, and said unto him, Abraham: and he said, Behold, here I am. And he said, Take now thy son, thine only son Isaac, whom thou lovest, and get thee into the land of Moriah; and offer him there for a burnt offering upon one of the mountains which I will tell thee of. Gen. 22:1-2.

This episode took place in a vision. According to Scripture, God often communicated with people in visions and dreams. "For God speaks once; he does not speak a second time; In a dream, in a vision of the night, when deep sleep falls upon men, while slumbering upon the bed . . ."[1] Most of God's communications with Abraham, Isaac, Jacob, and the prophets were in visions and dreams.

Abraham was living among many different tribal people who worshiped idols and even sacrificed their children to these deities. In those days, droughts, famines, plagues, and diseases were attributed to their tribal gods. Therefore, these people always tried to appease their various gods.

At that time, the land of Canaan had too many droughts, and people suffered from famines. Abraham saw some of these people sacrificing one or two of their children to their gods, so he thought he should do the same. After all, he was living in a pagan land. But it was revealed to him in a vision to offer a ram instead of his beloved son, Isaac. God tempts no one. "Let no man say when he is tempted, I am tempted of God; for God cannot be tempted with evil, and neither does he tempt any man."[2]

Abraham was to learn from his vision. This is why, in his dream, the Lord commanded Abraham to go to the land of Moriah in what is

---

[1]Job 33:14-15, Eastern Aramaic Peshitta text, Lamsa translation.
[2]James 1:13, Eastern Aramaic Peshitta text, Lamsa translation.

now Jerusalem. It is nearly a three day journey from Beer-sheba to Jerusalem, but in the vision it takes only a few minutes. The Eastern Aramaic text reads: "and go to the land of the Amorites." The word *Moriah* might be a corrupt form of the Semitic name *Amoriah.* The letter *aleph* in Semitic languages is a weak letter, and it is often silent or even omitted in writing.

When Abraham arrived in the land of the Amorites, he left the donkey with the servants, and he and his son Isaac went to the high place. Evidently, Abraham saw an altar on this high place and knew that this was the area of worship that God had indicated to him (see verses 5-6).

The actual location of the particular mountain or high place is unknown. The reason for this might be that the area of worship was so well-known that there was no need to point it out or to name it. The Amorites were a Semitic people. They must have had a site where they worshiped or a shrine on one of the high places to which tribal people went to proffer their burnt offerings.

In the book of Chronicles the place is called the Mountain of the Amorites, indicating that it was a shrine on one of the mountains. We suggest that the reference here is to Jerusalem, the Jebusite city where Solomon later built his great temple.[3]

Abraham had visited this city when he defeated the five Mesopotamian kings and when Melchizedek, the king of Salem (Aramaic: *Shalem*), the priest of the Most High God, brought him bread and wine and blessed him. Melchizedek also called Abraham the blessed of the God who was the possessor of heaven and earth.[4]

Like other Semitic tribes, the Amorites seemingly worshiped the God of heaven, the same living God to which Abraham went to sacrifice on this high place. This is why Abraham was told to go to the land of the Amorites.

Had Abraham, his son Isaac, and his servants actually traveled to Jerusalem, Melchizedek would have gone to greet Abraham, and

---

[3]2 Chron. 3:1.
[4]Gen. 14:18-19.

his princes and noblemen would have gathered around the altar for such a sacrifice. But there is no mention that Abraham was met by anyone. Nor is there any mention of Sarah, his wife.

Undoubtedly, Sarah would have protested against the sacrifice of her only beloved son, and she would have mourned for him. Again, this was a divine revelation to Abraham that took place in a vision. Abraham understood his divine dream, and God blessed him accordingly because he was willing to offer his son Isaac.[5]

A few days after, Abraham related his vision and its meaning, and from that day forward the Hebrews offered only sheep, rams, he-goats and oxen. Nevertheless, there are a few narratives where some of the Hebrew tribesmen offered human sacrifice.[6] Abraham learned that his God never wanted human sacrifices like the other tribal deities throughout the land of Canaan.

A Knife

And Abraham took the wood of the burnt offering, and laid it upon Isaac his son; and he took the fire in his hand, and a knife; and they went both of them together. Gen. 22:6.

This is probably the first mention of the word knife in Scripture.[7] Steel knives might have been a new invention and scarce. Sharp flint was used for circumcision.[8]

Iron and steel were in use a long time before Abraham. Noah would have had to have iron and steel tools in order to build such a large ship or ark. The Assyrians, Arameans, and Babylonians (Chaldeans) were great pioneers in all scientific fields. They had swords, chariots, and instruments of iron.

---

[5]Gen. 22:11-18.
[6]One incident is found in the book of Judges 11:34-39.
[7]See also Gen. 22:10.
[8]Ex. 4:25.

Figurative Speech

That in blessing I will bless thee, and in multiplying I will multiply thy seed as the stars of the heaven, and as the sand which is upon the seashore; and thy seed shall possess the gate of his enemies. Gen. 22:17.

These idiomatic expressions should not be taken literally. In biblical days, such large figures as millions and billions were unknown. A thousand, ten thousand, and hundreds of thousands were the highest numbers used by the learned men. The common people counted on their fingers and knew the familiar figures such as ten, twelve, twenty, forty and a hundred.

"As the stars of the heaven and as the sand which is upon the seashore" means "numerous" or " more than you can imagine." Of course, no one can count the stars or the sand. Literally speaking, the Hebrews have never been a numerous people like the Arabs, Chinese, Indians, and Russians.

But the descendants of Abraham are not only those of his posterity—that is, from his bloodline or lineage—but include those of the spirit also. All believers in the faith (religion) of Abraham are his descendants spiritually.[9]

---

[9]See Jn. 8:39, Gal. 3:7. See also the comment on Gen. 24:60, "Brides are Blessed," p. 146.

CHAPTER 23

Abraham a Prince

Hear us, my lord; thou art a mighty prince among us: in the choice of our sepulchres bury thy dead; none of us shall withhold from thee his sepulchre, but that thou mayest bury thy dead. Gen. 23:6.

Abraham was a God-revering man; he was also considered as a prince of God and venerated as a prophet. Abraham was the chief of a powerful tribe that defeated the five kings.[1]

Not only was Abraham a tribal chief, but he communed with God, received divine revelations, and gave counsel. These are the reasons he was revered by the native people throughout the region of Canaan.

Near Eastern Bargaining

Nay, my lord, hear me; the field give I thee, and the cave that is therein. I give it thee; in the presence of the sons of my people give I it thee: bury thy dead. Gen. 23:11.

In the Near East such statements and generosity are not taken seriously although the person might mean what he says. Near Easterners are habitually extravagant with their remarks, especially when buying and selling.

When a seller begins his conversation with a prospective customer, he may say: "It is yours; take it away!" or "My house is your home." But the customer knows they don't really mean what is being said.

As soon as the seller knows that the buyer is ready to buy, he

---

[1]Gen. 14:14-20.

then starts with a high price, and that is when the bargaining becomes serious.

In this case, there was no bargaining. Abraham's wife had died and she had to be buried. Ephron knew that Abraham was not going to bargain in the presence of mourners nor accept the burial ground gratis; and, being a prince, Abraham would not bury his wife in a burial plot that was not his. Abraham also knew the custom of the land and the business formalities. Even if Ephron might have meant what he said, he knew Abraham would not accept the field and the cave without paying for them. He also knew that Abraham would be willing to pay a higher price to avoid bargaining.[2]

Mature Men

Unto Abraham for a possession in the presence of the children of Heth, before all that went in at the gate of his city. Gen. 23:18.

"All that went in at the gate of his city" is an Aramaic idiom that means, "all mature men."[3] The elders spent most of their time at the gate of the city. Parks and other public places were not known in walled cities and towns.

Gates of the cities were used as places for public gatherings, loitering, and for conducting business or legal transactions.[4] At the gate of the city one could find friends, enemies, and business associates. War counsels were also held at the gate. Additionally, scribes and self-appointed judges were at the gates waiting to be called upon to perform services. This ancient custom was still practiced up until the 1930s, but it is no longer practiced.

---

[2]See also Gen. 25:9, 50:13.
[3]Gen. 23:10.
[4]Ruth 4:1-4, 1 Ki. 22:10.

CHAPTER 24

An Ancient Binding Oath

And Abraham said unto his eldest servant of his house, that ruled over all that he had, Put, I pray thee, thy hand under my thigh; And I will make thee swear by the Lord, the God of heaven and the God of the earth, that thou shalt not take a wife unto my son of the daughters of the Canaanites, among whom I dwell. Gen. 24:2-3.

The Eastern Aramaic text reads: ". . . under my girdle [*hasi*]." This Aramaic word has many meanings: "girdle, belt, loin, back." It also means, "to castrate, emasculate." In this case it refers to the belt that Near Easterners wore on their vests to keep their clothes together and prevent money, bread, and other articles from falling.

Placing one's hand under the girdle symbolizes a solemn and binding oath that cannot be broken. In some instances when people take an oath, they place their right hand on their heart. In the ancient days, the heart and kidneys were considered the most holy organs in the body.

This patriarchal admonition was later incorporated into the Mosaic laws and ordinances. The loyal Hebrews, or Israelites, refrained from marrying Gentile women or giving their daughters in marriage to Gentile men.

Just as a belt or girdle binds the clothes to the body, so the person is bound with the oath. Then again, the heart is close to the girdle.

Meeting at the Well

And he made his camels to kneel down without the city by a well of water at the time of the evening, even the time that women go out to draw water. Gen. 24:11.

Until recent times in the Near East, springs and wells were the only places where a man could see maidens or married women and converse with them. Near Easterners seldom looked at a strange woman and tried to converse with her. The father of a girl or the husband of a woman would have resented such repulsive behavior or advances.

Nevertheless, at a spring or at a well, one could carry on conversations with both girls and married women under the pretense of being thirsty and asking for water to drink.[1]

Young men purposely went to springs or wells during the evening hours to see the girls they loved and, if possible, to converse with them. Moses met his wife at a well,[2] and Jacob met Rachel at a well.[3] Semitic poets have composed many songs about lovers who met at a fountain or a well. When the disciples of Jesus of Nazareth saw that he was talking to the Samaritan woman at the well, they were surprised: ". . . and marveled that he talked with the woman."[4]

Abraham's servant trusted in his master's God, who knows all and ordains all. The Lord God led him to the right place at the right time, where he would meet the right woman who was to become the wife of his master's son. God guided him. Those who trust in the living God are willing to be directed by divine prompting.

Betrothal Custom

And there was set meat before him to eat: but he said, I will not eat, until I have told mine errand. And he said, Speak on. Gen. 24:33.

When Near Easterners went on a mission seeking the hand of a maiden for a bridegroom-to-be, they usually refused to eat or drink

---

[1]Gen. 24:45-46.
[2]Ex. 2:15-17.
[3]Gen. 29:2-12.
[4]Jn. 4:27.

until their request was granted and the father of the bride-to-be gave his consent.

On such occasions, generally in the evening, a party of respectable townsmen called on the father of the girl and, on their arrival, were greeted warmly and seated. Then food was set before them. But when they were asked to eat, they would decline. Then the father of the maiden would say to them, "You have come in peace; you have walked over my eyes," which meant, "You are most welcome." To this the chief matchmaker would reply: "May God bless you; may your eyes see more light." Then he would add: "We have come to seek the hand of your daughter." If the father is pleased, he says: "My daughter is a pair of shoes before your feet." Then the guests would begin to eat. But if he was unwilling to give his daughter in marriage, the guests would rise up, one by one, leaving the food on the table untouched.

Abraham's servant refused to eat until he saw that his mission had prospered and that Rebekah's father, Bethuel, and her brother, Laban, were willing to give her in marriage to their kinsman, Isaac. When Bethuel and his sons consented to give Rebekah to Isaac, then the engagement festivity began.[5]

Espousal Consent

And before I had done speaking in mine heart, behold, Rebekah came forth with her pitcher on her shoulder; and she went down unto the well, and drew water: and I said unto her, Let me drink, I pray thee. And she made haste, and let down her pitcher from her shoulder, and said, Drink, and I will give thy camels drink also: so I drank, and she made the camels drink also. Gen. 24:45-46.

When a maiden consented to give a drink to a prospective lover or an emissary of his, it indicated that she was willing to marry. The

---

[5]Gen. 24:51-54.

145

moment Abraham's servant saw that she was not only willing to give him a drink but also offered to give his camels a drink, he did not wait to see her father and brother; he put the earring on her ear and the bracelets on her arms.

Evidently, Rebekah must have been divinely informed regarding the man's mission. Both the servant and Rebekah were divinely guided because of the faith of Abraham and his loyalty to God. This success was not incidental or an accident, as may be seen from the story. Abraham believed in God and prayed for the success of his servant's mission and God granted him his request.

Brides are Blessed

And they blessed Rebekah, and said unto her, Thou art our sister; be thou the mother of thousands of millions, and let thy seed possess the gate of those which hate them. Gen. 24:60.

The numerical figure of "millions" was unknown to the ancients, just as the term "billion" was hardly known prior to World War II.

The ancient term used in this passage is *ribwatha*—that is, the great number "ten thousand." And the Aramaic expression *ribwath-ribwatha* means, "many ten thousands." At times, these figures were used without the slightest knowledge of the quantity. What they really meant was, "May you have many descendants."

When a girl is given in marriage, she is blessed by the priest and by her parents and relatives who wish her happiness, prosperity, and many children. Other figures of speech describing large numbers are: "sand of the sea," "leaves of the trees," and "stars of heaven."[6]

---

[6]See Gen. 22:17 and comment "Figurative Speech," p. 140.

What Rebekah had Done

And the servant told Isaac all things that he had done. Gen. 24:66.

The Eastern Aramaic text reads: "And the servant told Isaac all the things that she had done."[7] The Semitic letter *tau*, "t," at the end of a verb with two dots under it is the feminine ending. *Aiwdhat* is "she had done," not "he had done."

Rebekah gave Abraham's servant water to drink, and she also watered his camels.[8] The servant was relating to his master's son, Isaac, how God had prospered his way and answered his prayer, and how Rebekah had helped him and made her betrothal easy.

---

[7]Gen. 24:66, Eastern Aramaic Peshitta text, Lamsa translation.
[8]Gen. 24:18-22.

CHAPTER 25

Sheba and Dedan

And Jokshan begat Sheba, and Dedan. And the sons of Dedan were Asshurim, and Letushim, and Leummim. Gen. 25:3.

Sheba and Dedan were Abraham's great-grandsons from his wife Keturah. They were the grandsons of Zimran, Abraham's son. (Compare Genesis 10:7.)

Dedanites were kindred of the Midianites and other people who were descendants of Abraham, such as the Edomites and Amalekites. Many Arab tribes in western and southern Palestine trace their ancestry to Abraham. Many of these tribes lived in Teman, southern Palestine, known today as Negeb.[1] The Koresh, the most powerful Arab tribe in Mecca, traces its descendancy to Ishmael, the son of Abraham from Hagar.

Birthright

And Jacob said, Sell me this day thy birthright. Gen. 25:31.

In the Near East, the first-born is considered the heir of his father. He is the one who carries on with the family tradition; therefore, he receives the largest portion of his father's estate. In biblical days, the first-born received a double portion.[2]

Selling and buying of the birthright has nothing to do with God's blessing. Nevertheless, Near Easterners believe that such rights can be transferred from one person to another.

The little stew of lentils that Jacob gave to his brother Esau could

---

[1] Isa. 21:13-14, Jer. 25:23, Ezk. 27:20.
[2] Dt. 21:15-17.

not have changed God's mind. Jacob was preordained as the heir of his father, Isaac, by God. That is to say, God knew that Jacob was interested more in spiritual matters and in the family heritage than Esau was.

From his childhood, Esau was materially minded. As a man he was interested in hunting, fighting, and subduing other tribal people by means of his sword and bow. Therefore, he had disqualified himself as the heir of his father, Isaac. He was not concerned about his family's tribal destiny and the divine plan that ran through his family.

Rebekah knew that her elder son, Esau, was lenient toward other tribal gods and beliefs. But she also knew that her younger son, Jacob, was religiously inclined toward the faith of his grandfather, Abraham. The stew was incidental, but Isaac's teaching gave Jacob strength, wisdom, and a firm belief in the family religious tradition.

On the other hand, and according to the narrator, God chose Jacob simply because Jacob was the right man to carry on the spiritual tradition. God does not look to seniority nor is God partial. Human beings see only the outer appearance and make their judgments. But God knows the inner workings of the heart and mind of an individual.

CHAPTER 26

Satan

And they digged another well, and strove for that also; and he called the name of it Sitnah. Gen. 26:21.

The Eastern Aramaic text reads: "And they dug another well, and they quarreled over that also; and he called the name of it *Satana* [the adversary]."[1] This is the first time that the Aramaic term *Satana,* "Satan," is used. It means an "accuser, adversary." The term *Sitnah* is a verbal noun of the same root as "Satan" and means "adversity." The term "Satan" derives from the Aramaic root *sata,* "to mislead, go astray, slide, miss the mark." Anything that is deceitful, unjust, or contrary to truth is called "Satan" because it is misleading.

Isaac called the name of the well "Satan" simply because there had been so much contention, quarreling, and deception over it. The servants of Abimeleck, the king of Philistia, confiscated many of the good wells that the servants of Isaac had dug.

The other well over which they did not quarrel was called *rahboth,* "enlarge," because the servants of Abimleck did not contend with Isaac over this well.

A Prolific Well

And he called it Shebah: therefore the name of the city is Beer-sheba unto this day. Gen. 26:33.

Sabah in Aramaic means, "plenty, satisfied, filled." This word is different from *shebah,* meaning "seven."

Isaac called the name of the place *Beer-sbah,* the prolific well, the

---

[1]Gen. 26:21, Eastern Aramaic Peshitta text, Lamsa translation.

well with plenty of water. The words *sabah and shebah* are very similar. Previously, the place was named *Beer-shebah* by Abraham because he had dug seven wells.[2]

---

[2]See the comment on Genesis, Chapter 21:31, "Beer-Sheba," pp. 135-136.

CHAPTER 27

Esau's Special Garment

And Rebekah took goodly raiment of her eldest son Esau, which were with her in the house, and put them upon Jacob her younger son. Gen. 27:15.

In the Near East, all noble and rich men have an expensive suit that they wear at feasts, banquets, and other social and special occasions. Some of the parts of the garments are heavily embroidered, especially the sleeves. This good apparel is carefully stored by the women of the household to protect it from moths.

Esau was the firstborn and the heir of his father, Isaac. He was entitled to wear a special garment with long sleeves. Rebekah knew that her son Esau would wear his special garment on such an occasion and that Isaac might feel it with his fingers because his father's eyesight was failing him. This is the reason she put the garment on his son Jacob.

Jacob Means "Heel"

And he said, Thy brother came with subtilty, and hath taken away thy blessing. And he said, Is not he rightly named Jacob? And for he hath supplanted me these two times: he took away my birthright; and behold, now he hath taken away my blessing. Gen. 27:35-36.

In Aramaic, the name *Yacob,* "Jacob," derives from *ekba,* meaning "heel." When Jacob was born, his hand took hold of the heel of his twin brother, Esau.

According to the narrative, Esau and Jacob struggled together when they were in their mother's womb.[1] Years later, Esau thought that Jacob had held his heel in attempting to restrain or prevent him from being born first. Now Jacob had taken from him the birthright, the family blessing.

There is no doubt that Jacob was born to be the heir of his father, Isaac, and his grandfather, Abraham. Jacob was interested in the family traditions, culture, and religion; but Esau was only interested in hunting and diversions. It was Esau himself and his total disinterest in following the spiritual religion of the family that disqualified him from inheriting the rights as the firstborn and heir to the family.

---

[1]Gen. 25:22-23.

CHAPTER 28

Interpretation of Dreams

And he dreamed, and behold a ladder set up on the earth, and the top of it reached to heaven: and behold the angels of God ascending and descending on it. Gen. 28:12.

Jacob was skilled in dream interpretation. He was to become a tribal chief; therefore, he had to know how to interpret dreams for guidance, explain dark sayings, and how to lead a tribe in finding water and grazing for their flocks.

Isaac taught Jacob all the above skills in the same manner that Isaac's father, Abraham, had tutored him. In those days, this kind of knowledge was handed down from father to son. When Jacob had his son Joseph, by Rachel, he also taught him to interpret dreams and all other necessary matters in tribal leadership. He educated Joseph so well that, later on, this skill in dream interpretation would save Joseph's life and the lives of many other peoples. In the Near East, when dreams and visions become too difficult to interpret and understand, people seek God's help for their meaning.[1]

Jacob was fleeing from his brother, Esau, not knowing what the future had in store for him. While on his way to Padan-aram, he wondered if he would ever return to his people again. At dusk, when he arrived at a certain place, he decided to stop and pass the night. As he slept, Jacob had a vision. He saw angels ascending and descending a ladder that stood between heaven and earth.

According to Eastern dream interpretation, a ladder indicates an understanding or difficulties and challenges surmounted and overcome. In this instance, the angels (messengers) symbolized God's counsel. That is, Jacob was assured that he would be guided by divine messages and that the Lord God would change Esau's heart toward

---

[1]Dan. 9:20-24.

154

him and bring about a reconciliation between the two of them.

Jacob was to attain the highest success and prosperity in the land to which he was fleeing and later return to his family. He was going to return by the same way and to the same place where he saw the vision. This is why the angels were descending and ascending. There would be harmony. Heaven and earth were the two points of difference between Jacob and his twin brother, Esau, that would be bridged by understanding.

Pillars of Stone

And Jacob rose up early in the morning, and took the stone that he had put for his pillows, and set it up for a pillar, and poured oil upon the top of it. Gen. 28:18.

Prior to the Mosaic code of worship, sacred stones and trees were venerated and worshiped by the people. Many of the pagan altars were piles of stones or large rocks that had offered some protection to shepherds and travelers during the time of heat and severe storms. Trees also offered relief to thirsty and weary wayfarers.

Many of these ancient stones and trees that once were venerated are still to be found in northern Mesopotamia, Persia (Iran), and Arabia. Some people, even in modern times, respect these sacred stones and trees and visit them from time to time.

Jacob took the stone that he had used for his pillow and set it up for a pillar and consecrated it with oil. He did this as a memorial for the generations to come that they might not forget God's goodness and loving kindness to him and his posterity.

CHAPTER 29

Scarcity of Water

And they said, We cannot, until all the flocks be gathered together, and till they roll the stone from the well's mouth; then we water the sheep. Gen. 29:8.

In many regions of Palestine and Arabia where wells were not prolific, water was scarce and, at times, was rationed. People drew water in turns, and the flocks were watered together. The water was drawn in leather buckets and poured out into troughs constructed of stone or wood.

Shepherds obeyed the oral laws and respected the rights of their neighbors. Nevertheless, because of the scarcity of water, shepherds sometimes quarreled among themselves and killed one another. Moses, after his flight from Egypt, helped Jethro's daughters to water their sheep. He drove other shepherds away.[1]

Wages

And Laban said unto Jacob, Because thou art my brother, shouldest thou therefore serve me for naught? Tell me, what shall thy wages be? Gen. 29:15.

In those days, when silver and gold were scarce, both dowries and wages were paid in kind—that is, in sheep, cattle, salt, butter, and wheat—in many regions of Iran, Turkey, Arabia, and Palestine. This ancient custom was prevalent until World War I. Most of the business was transacted through the exchange of wheat, butter, cheese, hardware, rugs, and dry goods. During the first century CE in

---

[1]Ex. 2:16-17.

Palestine, some laborers were paid with money.[2]

The English word "salary" comes from the word "salt." During the Roman days, soldiers were paid with salt. Salt still remains a medium of exchange in a few areas of Africa. This is because in some of these regions salt is precious and difficult to obtain.

Charming and Attractive Eyes

Leah was tender eyed; Rachel was beautiful and well-favored.
Gen. 29:17.

The Aramaic word in this verse reads, *rakeekhan,* and it means, "pretty, warm, sparkling, attractive, charming, penetrating." Probably the error was caused by the confusion of the Semitic word *rateeban,* meaning, "weak, sick, watery," with *rekeekhan.*

In the appraisal, both girls were beautiful; one of them had attractive eyes, and the other was lovely, possessing a shapely, well built figure. In the Near East, many people overlooked the defects in a woman's body and pointed out the good qualities that she had.

Jacob chose Rachel simply because she was younger and he had met her first at the well and had fallen in love with her. Indeed, Leah's eyes were not weak or diseased as some biblical interpreters maintain. The eastern Aramaic text clearly reads that Leah had attractive eyes, but Rachel was beautiful and well favored.

A Dowry

And Jacob served seven years for Rachel; and they seemed unto him but a few days, for the love he had to her. And Jacob said unto Laban, Give me my wife, for my days are fulfilled, that I may go in unto her.
Gen. 29:20-21.

---

[2]See Mt. 20:2.

Even to this day, in the northern region of Mesopotamia that was ancient Assyria, some men pay a dowry to the father of the bride. The dowry is a very old custom and tradition, as old as the Bible itself. The dowry is paid in money, sheep, cattle, or labor. In that part of the world some people believe that when a man pays for his wife, he will appreciate and love her more.

Also, when a man pays a dowry, it makes divorce difficult. Jacob had neither money, sheep, nor cattle, so he had to pay his uncle by working for him.

In lower Mesopotamia, Syria, and Egypt, and in certain other regions, the father of the bride used to pay the prospective bridegroom for marrying his daughter. This is because there were more women than men.

Jacob Deceived by Laban

And it came to pass, that in the morning, behold it was Leah and he said to Laban, What is this thou hast done unto me? Did not I serve with thee for Rachel? Wherefore then hast thou beguiled me? Gen. 29:25.

In the Near East, honeymoons were unknown. After the wedding ceremonies and festivities, which generally lasted for several days, the bridegroom and the bride slept in the same room with the rest of the family. At times, there were more than ten families living under the same roof, and they all slept close to each other. In some homes the entire family slept in the same bed on the floor; privacy was unknown.

During the wedding feast, the bride's face was completely veiled and the bridegroom seldom had the opportunity to even see her. Also, during the wedding festivities, there is much confusion and drinking. Usually, after six or seven in the evening when it is dark, the lamps in the house are put out and everyone goes to bed. Not until the day breaks does the husband see the face of his wife with whom he has slept.

Jacob had seen Rachel clad in her wedding attire and also Leah serving and ministering to the guests. Therefore, he expected Rachel to be the one in bed with him. But his crafty uncle, Laban, had put Leah in the bed.

Jacob was shrewd, but Laban was even more clever than he. Now Laban made Jacob work seven more years for the girl he really loved. On the other hand, most of the Near Eastern fathers would refuse to give one of their younger daughters in marriage before the eldest was married. Customs and traditions were highly upheld in that part of the ancient world.

CHAPTER 30

Pleaded with Her

And Rachel said, With great wrestlings have I wrestled with my sister, and I have prevailed: and she called his name Naphtali. Gen. 30:8.

The Eastern Aramaic text reads: "And Rachel said: I besought the Lord, and pleaded with my sister, and I have attained my desire; and she called his name Naphtali."[1] The Aramaic term *Ethkashpaeth*, "I pleaded with her," means that Rachel had to obtain her sister's consent so that she could give her maid, Bilhah, to her husband, Jacob. The Aramaic word for "fought with her" or "wrestled with her" is *etkatshet*. These two words are so close that one may easily confuse one with the other.

Jacob's time was divided between Leah and Rachel. In lands where polygamy is still practiced, the husband visits each of his wives on their appointed day. Rachel had to plead with her sister so that her handmaid could sleep with Jacob. She wanted a child and was desperate to have this chance. Rachel's desire to have a child born from Bilhah prevailed. She had besought the Lord and through her handmaiden she had Dan and then later Bilhah bore another boy. Rachel named the second child Napthali.[2]

Black Sheep

And Jacob took him rods of green poplar, and of the hazel and chestnut tree; and pilled white strakes in them, and made the white appear which was in the rods. And he set the rods which he had piled before the flocks in the gutters in the watering troughs when the flocks came to drink,

---

[1] Gen. 30:8, Eastern Aramaic Peshitta text, Lamsa translation.
[2] See Gen. 30:1-8.

that they should conceive when they came to drink. Gen. 30:37-38.

As there is little use for black wool, black sheep were unwanted in the Near East. White wool could be dyed red, blue, green, yellow, and black. For Near Easterners, the color black was symbolic of death, mourning, and hardship.[3] People did not like this color. One could often hear people say: "My days have been black."

Invariably, there were a few black rams in the flocks because some of the families who made rugs liked the natural black wool more than the wool that had been dyed black. But most of the shepherds and sheep owners resented having black rams near their sheep during the mating seasons.

During the mating season, shepherds customarily borrowed rams from one another. On occasions, black rams were borrowed only when there was a need for black wool. When a shepherd wanted revenge against a family, he would let a black ram mate with white sheep belonging to that family.

How Jacob used the rods to achieve his purpose and to get even with his uncle, Laban, is challenging to understand. Thus far, no one has been able to duplicate this feat. Jacob knew a secret working with the rods. Jacob claimed that God had revealed it to him in a dream.[4]

God was with Jacob. Laban had tried to cheat him. The rods that Jacob used were immaterial in the incident. God needed no rods so that the white sheep might bear speckled and spotted lambs, but Jacob was to know that God was guiding and helping him. God was not a partner in any deceptive plan. Laban got what he deserved and Jacob was rewarded for his integrity, hard work, and faith in the God of his fathers.

---

[3]See Lam. 5:10 and Jude 1:13.
[4]Gen. 31:10-13.

161

CHAPTER 31

Women Purchased

Are we not counted of him strangers? For he hath sold us, and hath quite devoured also our money. Gen. 31:15.

In this passage, "he has sold us" means, "he has squandered our dowry." The Assyrian and Aramean fathers received a dowry for their daughters. Jacob worked fourteen years for Laban's daughters. And since Jacob married in Laban's house, his uncle gave his daughters no presents. Jacob's entire dowry of hard labor went to Laban.

A betrothed girl is called *makhirtha,* derived from *makhar,* "to purchase a wife" or "bargain for a wife." The imperfect form of the verb is *nmkhar* or *ymkhar.* Literally, the Aramaic word *makhirtha* means, "the purchased one." In Near Eastern liturgical books the church is called *makhirtheh damshikha.* The church is the bride, the purchased one of the Messiah/Christ, who has bought her with his blood—that is, his life.

Laban's Idol Gods

With whomsoever thou findest thy gods, let him not live: before our brethren discern thou what is thine with me, and take it to thee. For Jacob knew not that Rachel had stolen them. Gen. 31:32.

Jacob's father, Isaac, and his grandfather, Abraham, were worshipers of one God. Evidently, Abraham had left Ur of Chaldea simply because idolatry was prevalent. Seemingly, not all those who came with Abraham believed in one God, the God of heaven who had communed with him and commanded him to leave his kinsmen and his land and go into a land that God was going to show him. In other words, Abraham and his family may have been the only ones who

162

believed in one God. Nevertheless, God communed with the patriarchs or other families who had also forsaken their land and left with Abraham.

Laban was an idolater. His family had brought some of the images of their gods and goddesses with them. In those days, they used these idols and images to receive oracles, and they were often consulted by the leaders of the tribe. Gods were essential for tribal people because they needed good counsel during their migrations and grazing seasons, especially for their own welfare and for their livestock.

It seems that Jacob, even though he had prospered in Laban's house, worried over the presence of these idols and images. He preferred being with his people. All of the idol worship that was practiced in Laban's household made him long to return to his own people. Jacob was not interested in these gods and never knew that his wife, Rachel, had stolen some of the images from Laban, her father.

Cold and Heat

Thus I was in the day the drought consumed me, and the frost by night: and my sleep departed from mine eyes. Gen. 31:40.

The temperature in the northern region of the Arabian desert rises as high as 120 degrees during the day and falls as low as 55 degrees during the night. Shepherds who tend their flocks during the day and watch over them at night suffer from both heat and cold. Faithful shepherds sleep little during the night because thieves steal at night time, and wild animals strike when the shepherd is asleep.

In the Near East, when people say, "I was frozen," they simply mean that they were cold. During certain times of the year one can find frost on the ground, yet during the day the temperature of standing water may be very high.

Jacob had been faithful to his father-in-law, Laban, and had undergone many hardships and made many sacrifices in order to make good. But his father-in-law had not been fair to him. He had treated him as an employee.

Heap of Stones

And Laban called it Jegar-sahadutha: but Jacob called it Galeed. And Laban said This heap is a witness between me and thee this day. Therefore was the name of it called Galeed; And Mizpah; for he said, The Lord watch between me and thee, when we are absent one from another.
Gen. 31:47-49.

The Aramaic phrase reads: *yaghra dsahdutha,* "the heap of witness." Jacob also called it in his dialect *Gilaadh,* "the pillar of witnessing;" that is, the witness to a covenant. The heap of stones was to remain as a witness to the agreement between Laban and Jacob. *Dokta* in Aramaic means "watchman." In Hebrew it is rendered *mizpah,* "watch."

Mizpeh in Aramaic means, "Let the Lord settle the problems between you and me." Laban had tried to cheat Jacob, but Jacob also was not entirely innocent toward his father-in-law. In a clever manner, Jacob had been able to acquire most of his father-in-law's flocks.[1]

The pillar of stones was built as an everlasting witness to the agreement that was made between Laban and his nephew and son-in-law, Jacob. When the heap was built, then they sacrificed sheep, ate the meat, and celebrated their covenant. According to the biblical episode, Laban had been divinely warned not to do any harm to Jacob. The pillar of stones was also a reminder that Jacob must not despise or mistreat Laban's daughters, and Laban was never to seek vengeance against Jacob for his conduct.

The heap became a boundary line between Laban's and Jacob's

---

[1]Gen. 30:37-43.

descendants. Neither side was ever to transgress this agreement. Years later, Gilead became a disputed borderland between Israel and Syria.

GALEED

The term in Aramaic is *Gil-aadh,* in Hebrew *Gilead* or *Gal-ed.* It is a compound noun, *Gil-adad,* which means, "the gully of meeting, celebrating, witnessing, and affirming of agreement." Galeed is a mountainous country with many valleys and ravines.

Laban used the term *sadutha* with Jacob, which derives from *sahad,* meaning "to bear witness" to the agreement that was just concluded between them. Jacob and Laban met and celebrated in this historic land, and each one gave a different name to the place. The Semitic term *Galeed* or *Gilead* was known to the Israelites prior to the Exodus. "And Machir begat Geilead."[2] Galeed lies between the Sea of Galilee and the Dead Sea. On the east of Galeed is the desert and on the south, Moab.

Prior to the occupation of the land of Canaan by Joshua, Galeed was under the rule of Sihon, the king of the Amorites, who dwelt east of the Jordan, the territory between Arnon and Jabbok and between Jabbok and the Yarmuk.

This mountainous land was given by Moses to the tribes of Reuben and Gad and to half of the tribe of Manasseh. These tribes had large flocks and herds. In Arabia it is called Jaladah.

---

[2]Num. 26:29.

CHAPTER 32

Presents to Appease

And say, ye moreover, Behold, thy servant Jacob is behind us. For he said, I will appease him with the present that goeth before me, and afterward I will see his face; peradventure he will accept of me. Gen. 32:20.

In the Near East, when princes, governors, generals, and rulers entered a city, they were met by a welcoming party and greeted with lavish presents of silver, gold, sheep, oriental rugs, and other valuable things.

In biblical days, when these high rulers and officials were angry with the inhabitants of a town, people would bring them presents to appease and abate their anger. Through their gifts they would secure favors from these officials. "Every one loveth gifts [bribes]."[1]

Gifts were also offered to judges and governors for favors. "And thou shalt take no gift: for the gift blindeth the wise and perverteth the words of the righteous."[2] The recipient prefers to call it a "present."

Wrestling with an Angel

And Jacob was left alone; and there wrestled a man with him until the breaking of the day. Gen. 32:24.

The news that Esau, Jacob's twin brother, was on his way to meet him, accompanied by four hundred men, had caused Jacob considerable anxiety and fear. He could not tell how Esau would react when they encountered each other. Therefore, Jacob kept pondering

---

[1]Isa. 1:23.
[2]Ex. 23:8.

his past, such as the ways in which he had stolen the blessings from his brother. So that evening, Jacob had a night vision in which he wrestled not with an angel but with a man; that is, the wrestling was between Jacob and his brother Esau.

Esau was a noble man and had not done any wrong to Jacob. He had put the shortcomings and double dealings of his brother out of his mind. He let go of the hurtful past; in other words, Esau was like an angel. When Esau declined to accept Jacob's present, the latter said to him: ". . . because now I have seen your face, as I saw the face of an angel, and you were pleased with me."[3]

Heavenly angels have no physical bodies with which to wrestle and fight. The physical strain that occurred in Jacob's hip when wrestling with the man was probably created from the mental and emotional disturbances in his mind. His hip was not dislocated. Jacob's vision was very traumatic. It was a psychosomatic illness brought about through the fear and regret over his unfair dealings with Esau.

The Term Israel

And he said, Thy name shall be called no more Jacob, but Israel: for as a prince hast thou power with God and with men, and hast prevailed. Gen. 32:28.

"*Israel*" is an Assyrian name that means "prince of God." *Sar* means "prince," and *Ael* or *El* means "God." *Jacob* in Aramaic means "heel." The name Jacob was given to him because during the time of his birth, he was holding his twin brother's heel. Now in his vision, when Jacob strove with the messenger and prevailed, the angel said to him, "Your name shall be called no longer Jacob, but Israel."

For many centuries all of the twelve tribes (sons) that came from

---

[3]See Gen. 33:10 and 32:25-30, Aramaic Peshitta text, Lamsa translation. The term "angel" means "messenger."

Jacob were collectively called Israel. Later, when Israel conquered the land of Canaan and settled under a monarchy, the ten northern tribes split from the two southern tribes, Judah and Benjamin, and became known as the house of Israel. The term "Judah" or "House of Judah" was only used when people referred to the two tribes of Judah and Benjamin. Judah, of course, was the predominate tribe in the South.

During the time of the conquest of Palestine and the period of the Judges, the term "Israel" was used as a national name, like Edom (Esau), Moab, and Ammon. Then, when the monarchy was established in Israel, Saul became king over the twelve tribes.

But after the division of the kingdom during the reign of Rehoboam, the son of Solomon, when the ten tribes left the house of David and the tribe of Judah, the term "Israel" was used only when referring to the ten tribes, whose capital was Samaria. Judah and Benjamin were the two tribes who remained loyal to the house of David.

After the destruction of the first temple and the Babylonian captivity, the remnant of the people who were left in the land of Israel were known as "Jews." This is because political Israel and Judah had come to an end, and now the people were known by their faith. They were called "Jews" simply because the center of worship was in the south, Jerusalem, and in the state of Judea. Therefore, the term "Jews" is solely religious. Anyone who embraces the Jewish faith can be called a Jew but cannot be called an Israelite or a Hebrew.

CHAPTER 33

Gifts Declined

And he said, What meanest thou by all this drove which I met? And he said, These are to find grace in the sight of my lord. And Esau said, I have enough my brother; keep that thou hast unto thyself. Gen. 33:8-9.

Customarily, Near Easterners decline gifts when they are offered, merely for politeness. When a gift is offered, the recipient will refuse to accept it, stating that he has plenty and thanks the giver; but he knows that the presenter will ask him again and again to receive the gift. The more an individual declines, the more he will be urged to accept.

Jacob urged his brother Esau to accept his gift not so much because of the Near Eastern custom but because he wanted to pacify him. Had Esau refused to receive the gift, Jacob would never have been at peace with his brother. A refusal to accept the gift meant permanent enmity. Esau, sooner or later, would have sought vengeance against his brother.

Jacob's received gift was a token of reconciliation, understanding, and an everlasting peace bond between them. The gift healed the wound and repaired the breach that was created by jealousy.

Esau an Angel

And Jacob said, Nay, I pray thee, if now I have found grace in thy sight, then receive my present at my hand: for therefore I have seen thy face, as though I had seen the face of God, and thou wast pleased with me. Gen. 33:10.

According to the biblical narrative, before Jacob had seen his

169

brother Esau, he was worried and restless. He had spent most of the night by the brook Jabbok in prayer and supplication. As Jacob fell asleep and began dreaming, he saw himself wrestling with an angel; and the contest continued all night till dawn.[1]

The entire dream was symbolic. The angel with whom Jacob was wrestling was his brother Esau. Through this night vision, the Lord had answered Jacob's prayers and revealed the matter to him. Esau had been bitter and hostile toward Jacob, but now he had made his mind up to attempt a reconciliation with his brother and to welcome him. After all, they were twins.

Angel in Aramaic means "God's counsel." It also means someone who is innocent and good. In the Near East, innocent and pious men are often referred to as angels. Esau was innocent like an angel.

Just as the angel blessed Jacob in his vision, so Esau kissed his twin brother. He also embraced him and received Jacob's gift of reconciliation. "A gift is as a precious stone."[2]

Jacob acted wisely when presenting himself to Esau as "your servant, Jacob," and by bowing to him seven times.

---

[1]Gen. 32:24.
[2]Prov. 17:8.

CHAPTER 34

Devious Deception

And Shechem said unto her father and unto her brethren, Let me find grace in your eyes, and what ye shall say unto me I will give. Ask me never so much dowry and gift, and I will give according as ye shall say unto me: but give me the damsel to wife. Gen. 34:11-12.

The Aramaic text reads: "And Shechem said to her father and to her brothers, Let me find mercy in your presence, and what ever you shall ask of me I will give. Ask me as much as you wish, both dowry and gifts, and I will give you according as you shall say to me, but give me this girl to wife. And the sons of Jacob answered Shechem and Hamor his father deceitfully, because they[1] had defiled Dinah their sister. And they said to them, We cannot do this thing, to give our sister to a man who is uncircumcised; for that would be a reproach to us; But on this condition will we consent to you: that you will become like us, and circumcise every male as we are circumcised."[2]

A dowry is an ancient Near Eastern custom as old as the Bible itself. In many regions of the Near East, a dowry is paid in kind to the father of the damsel—either a sum of money, or cattle, or sheep. Semites believe the father and mother of the daughter are entitled to a dowry, and some believe that the husband, by paying the dowry, will prize and treasure his wife more. A dowry is the value of the girl.[3]

Shechem was willing to pay whatever value Jacob and his sons demanded of him. But Jacob's sons lied to the men of Shechem and

---

[1]See Gen. 34:2. The "they" in the verse refers to Shechem and his father Hamor although it was Schechem himself who defiled Dinah.

[2]Gen. 34:11-15, Eastern Aramaic Peshitta text, Lamsa translation.

[3]See the comment on Gen. 29:20-21, "A Dowry," pp.157-158.

171

instead of asking for the dowry, they asked that all the men of the town become circumcised so that they might weaken all the adult men and slay them.

PRICE OF A BRIDE

The Aramaic term *mahra* and the Hebrew and Arabic *mahar* mean "the price of the marriage settlement."[4] *Mahar* is to be distinguished from the gift of the bridegroom to the bride, or the dowry that was brought by the bride from her wealthy father's house.[5]

In the ancient Near East, the law of the dowry was influenced by the scarcity or the abundant availability of women. Where the marriageable women were scarce, and according to the Assyrian law, the bridegroom paid the father of the bride; but in Mesopotamia and some other countries, where women were more numerous, the father of the bride paid the groom. (In the mountainous regions, women are scarce; but in the plains males are scarce.)

ADULT MALES

In verse 24, the Aramaic text reads: "And when all the adults of the town had heard from Shechem and from his father Hamor, they circumcised every male, those that went out of the gate of his town."[6] The phrase "those that went out of the gate" is an Aramaic idiomatic expression of speech that means "all the grown men" and not the little boys.[7] Simeon and Levi, two sons of Jacob, were planning to take each man his sword and quietly enter the town so that they could slay every adult male. When they did this atrocity, Simeon and Levi also slew Hamor and Shechem with the edge of the sword and took Dinah out of Shechem's house. After the slaughter was completed, the sons

---

[4] For the idea of a dowry see Ex. 22:16 and 1 Sam. 18:25.
[5] Jos. 15:18.
[6] Gen. 34:24, Eastern Aramaic Peshitta text, Lamsa translation.
[7] See Gen. 23:18, "Mature Men," p. 142.

of Jacob came back to the slain and plundered the town. These brothers felt justified in doing such an act because Shechem had defiled their sister, Dinah. So they took sheep, oxen, donkeys, and whatever was in the town and in the field. They also took all their wealth, and little ones and the wives of the slain men were also taken captive. The devious deception of Jacob's sons was played out.

Meeting Places

And Hamor and Shechem his son came unto the gate of their city, and communed with the men of their city. Gen. 34:20.

In the Near East, the gates of the walled towns and cities were used for playgrounds, meetings, and judgment sites. This is because the streets were narrow, and parks and public places were unknown.

CHAPTER 35

Alien Gods

And they gave unto Jacob all the strange gods which were in their hand, and all their earrings which were in their ears; and Jacob hid them under the oak which was by Shechem. Gen. 35:4.

These alien deities were images that their ancestors had brought from Padan-aram. The people in Mesopotamia worshiped many gods, just as Abraham's ancestors did in Ur of Chaldea.

The earrings were talismans and bore emblems of the foreign deities. These ornaments were a stumbling block to the people, who were surrounded by many idolatrous and corrupt tribal people. Jacob wanted his people to cleanse themselves of all pagan cultic images.

Oak of Weeping

But Deborah Rebekah's nurse died, and she was buried beneath Bethel under an oak; and the name of it was called Allon-bachuth. Gen. 35:8.

Bitmtha dawkhatha means "the oak of weeping." *Bitmtha* sometimes means "terebinth." This name was given as a memorial to Deborah, Rebekah's nurse, who was buried under the oak. The report of Deborah's death was an indication of the severing of all the old ties with alien gods and beliefs. Jacob was returning to Bethel with his people cleansed of all past associations with pagan elements. That is the reason why Deborah's death was mentioned. She represented a closing of the past era.

Son of My Right Hand

And it came to pass, as her soul was in departing, (for she died,) that she called his name Ben-oni; but his father called him Benjamin. Gen. 35:18.

The Eastern Aramaic text reads: "And it happened that as her soul was departing and she was dying, she called the child's name *Bar-kaebai* (Son of My Sorrow); but his father named him *Binyamin* (Son of My Right Hand)."[1] Jacob loved Rachel more than Leah and always thought of her children as his heirs.

"Right hand" in Aramaic is very meaningful. It signifies trust, loyalty, and power. For one to sit on the right hand of a king was a very high honor; it meant complete trust and power."To sit on the right hand of God" meant all power.[2]

Reuben's Deliberate Violation

And Israel journeyed, and spread his tent beyond the tower of Edar. And it came to pass, when Israel dwelt in that land, that Reuben went and lay with Bilhah, his father's concubine and Israel heard it. Gen 35:21-22.

Bilhah was Rachel's maid. Rachel gave her maid to Jacob as a substitute wife because she was having difficulty in becoming pregnant and was humiliated by her sister, who was bearing children for Jacob.[3] The two sons by Bilhah were Dan and Napthali.

Reuben (Rubel in Aramaic) was Jacob's firstborn son by his first wife, Leah. Reuben's sexual assault on Bilhah was an act of rebellion against his father's authority. Although by birthright Reuben was to inherit everything from his father, he prematurely claimed this right

---

[1]Gen. 35:18, Eastern Aramaic Peshitta text, Errico.
[2]See Mk. 16:19.
[3]Gen. 30:1-8.

by defiling Bilhah. The co-habitation also lessened Bilhah's status and competition with his mother, Leah. He wanted to make sure his mother would not be rivaled by Bilhah and not suffer any humiliation. Jacob always favored Rachel and her children above everyone else. Reuben was attempting to usurp leadership over the entire twelve tribes. However, his deliberate act would cause him to lose his rightful place in the inheritance.[4] There are several biblical narratives of this nature that are recorded in Scripture.[5]

---

[4]Gen. 49:3-4 and 1 Chron. 5:1.
[5]2 Sam. 3:7-8 and 1 Ki. 2:13-25.

CHAPTER 37

Coat of Long Sleeves

And it came to pass, when Joseph was come unto his brethren, that they stript Joseph out of his coat, his coat of many colours that was on him. Gen. 37:23.

The Eastern Aramaic text reads: *koteena dpidhyatha,* "coat of long sleeves." These coats or *abayas* are generally worn by princes, noblemen, and learned men. The sleeves and front parts of the garment are embroidered with silk of diverse colors. Thus, the color is in the embroidery of the garment and not in the material itself.

Princes and noblemen never work; therefore, they are attired with a garment of long sleeves. This is a token of honor, dignity, and the position they occupy in society. On the other hand, a poor man can neither afford such a coat with long sleeves, nor can he work while wearing a garment of this style.

Joseph was tutored by his father, Jacob, to succeed him as the head of the tribe. Joseph was elevated to the rank of a crown prince and a scholar. Reuben, the firstborn and rightful heir, had defiled his father's bed, violating Bilhah, the concubine who served Rachel. By the defiant act, Reuben was challenging his father's authority. Jacob's other sons were not suited to be tutored for this high office as chief of the tribe, which was a political, religious, and judicial position.

It was Jacob who had taught Joseph to interpret dreams and sit in council and manage tribal affairs. In addition to this, the chief must find grazing places for the flocks and cattle of the entire tribe. He must provide wells, make treaties with the chiefs of other tribes, and lead his people to war if necessary. He must know something about law and religion, read the stars for navigation in the desert, be ready for weather changes, interpret dreams, and many other matters that are essential for the welfare of a nomad tribe. In these lands people depend on wells for water, migrate by means of the stars, and communicate one with the other through dreams and visions.

Joseph was the only one among the sons of Jacob who could occupy such a position, so his brothers were jealous of him. All of them except Benjamin were older than he. The very fact that his father had given him such a garment of honor proved that he had selected him to take his place and that he was teaching him all the skills that he would need as chief of the tribe.

Ishmaelites and Midianites

Then there passed by Midianites merchantmen; and they drew and lifted up Joseph out of the pit, and sold Joseph to the Ishmaelites for twenty pieces of silver: and they brought Joseph into Egypt. Gen. 37:28.

The reference here is to the descendants of Ishmael, the son of Abraham, who was a relative to Jacob and his sons. The Midianites also were descendants of Abraham.[1] Both tribes were Hebrews in origin. They traveled together for protection from their enemies, the Amorites, Hittites, and other tribal peoples, who were the early inhabitants of Canaan. Both the Ishmaelites and Midianites spoke the same language—that is, the Aramaic tongue that their father, Abraham, and his tribe had brought from Haran and from Ur of Chaldea.

There were only three generations of Ishmaelites in the land, but they were a strong people, who exerted a tremendous influence over the native peoples. In a short space of time, they became princes and rulers over other tribes whose culture and religions were not as unified or powerful as those of the Hebrew tribe. The Ishmaelites might have been the leaders of the caravan. Being a warrior people, they were greatly feared by the weaker tribes in Canaan.

---

[1] Gen. 25:2

CHAPTER 38

Ceased Bearing

And she yet again conceived, and bare a son; and called his name Shelah: and he was at Chezib, when she bare him. Gen. 38:5.

The Eastern Aramaic text reads: "And she conceived again, and bore a son; and he called his name Shelah; and after she bore him she stopped bearing."[1] "He was at Chezib" is not present in the Aramaic text.

The Aramaic word *pisqath* means, "she stopped bearing." In Aramaic, when a woman ceases bearing children, people say:"She is cut off from bearing."

Shuah bore three sons to Judah, but she stopped having children after the birth of Shelah.

Birth Control

And Judah said unto Onan, Go in unto thy brother's wife, and marry her, and raise up seed to thy brother. And Onan knew that the seed should not be his; and it came to pass, when he went in unto his brother's wife, that he spilled it on the ground, lest that he should give seed to his brother. And the thing which he did displeased the Lord; wherefore he slew him also. Gen. 38:8-10.

Semitic people, from the very beginning, believed that the continuity of life was in posterity. When a man died without a son, he was cut off from life eternal. Therefore, when a man dies without an heir, the brother of the deceased marries the widow to raise an heir for him.

---

[1]Gen. 38:5, Eastern Aramaic Peshitta text, Lamsa translation.

Onan was unwilling to raise an heir for his brother who had died. He knew that the heir would be a rival to him as generally happens. This is the reason Onan practiced a very ancient form of birth control.

The continuance of life is not in posterity or in the individual but in the survival of the race. Millions of men have sacrificed their lives for the sake of their country and left no posterity. Martyrs and saints also have given their lives so that others could live. Certainly these people are not going to be cut off from the tree of life because of not having any children. Not all branches in a tree produce fruit, but all of the branches share in nourishing the fruits.

In those days, everything was attributed to God because they believed nothing could happen without God's knowledge. When Onan took ill, the people believed it was because God was displeased with him for not raising an offspring for his brother and, therefore, Onan's death was attributed to God. It was the writer of the text who believed that God slew Onan. God does not slay people. God is the way of salvation for all humanity.

Unwritten Law

When Judah saw her, he thought her to be a harlot; because she had covered her face. And he turned unto her by the way, and said, Go to I pray thee, let me come in unto thee; (for he knew not that she was his daughter-in-law.) And she said, What wilt thou give me, that thou mayest come in unto me? Gen. 38:15-16.

When Tamar saw that Onan refused to let her have a child from him and that her father-in-law, Judah, had not given her to Shelah, she disguised herself and covered her face. She must have a child, an heir for her deceased husband. Tamar, by veiling her entire head and face, was able to deceive Judah. He did not know that he was about to have intercourse with his daughter-in-law.

Although the Mosaic law came four hundred years later, there was an unwritten moral code among the tribes. People considered it

180

evil to marry a close relative. Pharaoh reproached Abraham for having told him that Sarah was his sister instead of his wife. The same situation arose with Isaac when he lied to Abimelech about Rebekah. Jacob also never forgave his firstborn son, Reuben, because he cohabited with one of his concubines.

During this time, women were punished with death when breaking the unwritten moral code. This was before the Mosaic law was revealed, and immoral actions were punished with death. Had Tamar not taken Judah's ring, robe, and staff as a pledge, she would have been burned alive. But Tamar was clever. Judah realized that he was at fault for the entire matter and confessed it to everyone. He knew that he should have given Tamar in marriage to his son, Shelah.

A Giant

And it came to pass, as he drew back his hand, that, behold, his brother came out; and she said, How hast thou broken forth? This breach be upon thee: therefore his name was called Pharez. Gen. 38:29.

Pharez, or *Pheriz,* in colloquial Aramaic means, "a mighty man" or "a giant." The child was named Pharez simply because he prevailed against his brother, Zarah. The midwife expected the latter to be born first, but Pharez was born first. Pharez is the ancestor of the kings of Judah.

CHAPTER 40

Dreams

And they said unto him, We have dreamed a dream, and there is no interpreter of it. And Joseph said unto them, Do not interpretations belong to God? Tell me them, I pray you. Gen. 40:8.

In the ancient days, the chief occupation of the wise and learned was to interpret dreams, explain riddles and dark sayings, and to foretell things to come. This knowledge was handed down from father to son and from a teacher to his student. Assyrians, Chaldeans, and Egyptians had astrologers, soothsayers, and interpreters of dreams and visions.

Abraham, Isaac, and Jacob communed with God by means of dreams, visions, and revelations, and they understood the meaning of the symbols they saw in their dreams. Jacob, on his way to Padan-aram, when fleeing from his brother, Esau , saw a ladder set on earth and the top of it reached to the sky. According to the book of Job, visions and dreams were some of the ways that God communicated with people. "For God speaks once; he does not speak a second time; In a dream, in a vision of the night, when deep sleep falls upon men, while slumbering upon the bed; Then he opens the ears of men, and humbles them according to their rebelliousness."[1] Joseph was tutored by his father, Jacob, and excelled as a dream interpreter.

---

[1] Job 33:14-16, Eastern Aramaic Peshitta text, Lamsa translation.

CHAPTER 41

Magicians

And it came to pass in the morning that his spirit was troubled; and he sent and called for all the magicians of Egypt, and all the wise men thereof; and Pharaoh told them his dream; but there was none that could interpret them unto Pharaoh. Gen. 41:8.

In biblical days, magicians and wise men were employed as counselors to kings and statesmen. Magic was a highly regarded profession, and magicians were greatly honored by kings and princes. The magicians also performed feats of magic in kings' palaces to entertain the idle and bored potentates.

Egyptian magicians were noted for their skills. Magic was a great and important art in Egypt. Even priests were great magicians because magic played a conspicuous part in their temple rituals.

However, the Egyptians were not as well versed in the interpretation of dreams and visions. This was a totally different field of study that was common among the tribal people who dwelt in the deserts, but unknown to highly cultured wise men of Egypt, who relied on human wisdom more than the hidden power of God.

The Israelites could foretell future events and predict years of famine and prosperity, but the art of magic was unknown to them. In other words, they were a simple, nomadic people, who relied on a spiritual power. This is the reason the wisdom of Joseph and Moses was greater than that of the Egyptians.

Like Moses and Aaron, the Egyptian magicians performed many wonders, but the wonders performed by Moses and Aaron were divinely guided.

A Double Dream

And for that the dream was doubled unto Pharaoh twice; It is because the thing is established by God, and God will shortly bring it to pass. Gen. 41:32.

The fact that the dream was doubled indicated to Pharaoh that the matter he had seen was very important and was to happen soon. In the Near East, when a matter is serious, the words are repeated for emphasis.

In a dream one might forget certain symbols but cannot easily forget all of them. If Pharaoh should forget the dream of seven cows, he would remember the dream of seven ears of wheat or vice versa.

Even in modern times many Near Easterners have been guided by dreams and visions they see, and they know the meaning of the symbols.[1]

Rings

And Pharaoh took off his ring from his hand, and put it upon Joseph's hand, and arrayed him in vestures of fine linen, and put a gold chain about his neck. Gen. 41:42.

The custom of wearing rings and other gold and silver ornaments is as old as the history of humankind. Kings, princes, governors, and noblemen wore rings as a symbol of authority, wealth, and power. Rings were also indispensable articles in marriage. They were given as a token of the agreement. Rings, earrings, and bracelets were given to brides as a sign of affection and love from their spouses.[2] Also, rings were used as signets wherewith imperial edicts, secret documents, and treaties were sealed.[3]

---

[1]See the comment on Gen. 28:12, pp. 154-155.
[2]Gen. 24:30, 53.
[3]Esther 3:12; Dan. 6:17.

The Israelites used rings, earrings, bracelets, and other jewelry more than any other tribal people. Such articles were indispensable in their society. They were worn on fingers, ears, and ankles.[4]

Lifting of Hand

And Pharaoh said unto Joseph, I am Pharaoh, and without thee shall no man lift up his hand or foot in all the land of Egypt. Gen. 41:44.

"Lift up his hand or foot" is an Aramaic idiom which means, "no one shall start to do anything without your approval." Such idioms are derived from the customs and manners of the people. In the Near East during Dr. Lamsa's time, most of the labor was done with the hands and feet.

Joseph's position was similar to a vizier of the Arabian empire. He was second to the emperor and had unlimited powers and authority over the people, so much so that no one dared to do anything in government without his consent or to question his wisdom and understanding.

Zaphnath-paaneah

And Pharaoh called Joseph's name Zaphnath-paaneah; and he gave him to wife Asenath the daughter of Potiphe-rah priest of On. And Joseph went out over all the land of Egypt. Gen. 41:45.

Zaphnath-paaneah (Aramaic: *panakh*) means, "the interpreter of dreams" or "revealer of hidden secrets." It may also mean, "the savior of the world." Joseph saved Egypt and many other lands during the severe famine. As an interpreter of dreams, he was made the chief of astrologers and soothsayers.

---

[4]Isa. 3:18-23.

CHAPTER 43

Gifts for Officials

*And their father Israel said unto them, If it must be so now, do this;
take of the best fruits in the land in your vessels, and carry down the man
a present, a little balm, and a little honey, spices and myrrh, nuts and
almonds.* Gen. 43:11.

When Semites called on a prince, a high government official, or
a holy man, they presented gifts to him, not always as a bribe but
sometimes as a token of honor and respect. This custom is so old and
widely practiced that princes, judges, and government officials expect
some kind of gift from their visitors. To call on them with empty
hands is disrespectful, and some of them would be offended. "And
the daughter of Tyre shall be there with a gift."[1]

A gift should not be confused with *shukhda,* "a bribe." The term
"bribe" is often translated in the King James as "gift." "For a gift does
blind the eyes of the wise, and pervert the words of the righteous."[2]

Jacob's gift was not a bribe but a present that was expected by
high government officials such as Joseph, who was governor general
over all the land of Egypt.

Religious Differences

*And they set on for him by himself, and for them by themselves, and
for the Egyptians, which did eat with him, by themselves because the
Egyptians might not eat bread with the Hebrews; for that is an abomination
unto the Egyptians.* Gen. 43:32.

---

[1]Ps. 45:12, K. J. V.
[2]Dt. 16:19, K. J V. See also Ex. 23:8.

In many Near Eastern countries, members of one religion refuse to eat a meal with the members of another religion. In some regions, Jews, Muslims, and Christians cannot eat together.

Bread is symbolic of friendship; therefore, only those who are on good terms with one another can sit at the same table and break bread together. When two men eat bread and salt together, they consider themselves friends. But the followers of rival religions cannot be friends; therefore, they cannot eat bread together. If they do, then they are not truly loyal to their religion. One often hears people saying to one another: "He ate my bread and yet he has done me harm."

Since the Hebrews were a pastoral people, they ate only certain kinds of animal meats, such as sheep, which the Egyptians considered to be an abomination.[3]

Near Eastern Etiquette

And they sat before him, the firstborn according to his birthright, and the youngest according to his youth: and the men marveled one at another. Gen. 43:33.

From time immemorial, Semites have revered and respected gray hairs and seniority. The younger salutes the older and lets him occupy a higher seat at a banquet or a religious feast. At times the younger men stand up while in the presence of their elders.

In the ancient Near East, chairs and tables were unknown. Desert people and their guests sat upright on the floor, with their legs folded under them, around the cloth that is spread before them. Each person is seated according to his age; the honored guests recline against bedding and cushions.

Jacob's sons were brought up well mannered and tutored by their father. Their fathers and grandfathers had feasted with princes and kings. The tribal people were taught to respect the chiefs of the tribes

---

[3]Gen. 46:34.

and the elders who acted as counselors and to behave properly in the presence of rulers. The Egyptians were amazed because they did not expect that these desert and semi-nomadic men would know anything about good manners.

Exchanging and Sharing Food

And he took and sent messes unto them from before him; but Benjamin's mess was five times so much as any of theirs. And they drank, and were merry with him. Gen. 43:34.

At a feast or a banquet the best dishes containing delicacies are customarily placed before the host and the honored guests who are seated at the table close to him.

During the meal the host or some of the honored guests take food from the special dishes that are before them and pass them to their friends. The sops of food are wrapped in thin bread and exchanged without hesitation or embarrassment.

At times, a man may taste a sop by eating a portion of it and then pass the rest to one of the guests near him. Semites are not afraid of germs. In the Near East, to exchange food, sops, and to eat from one another's dish is a great honor and a sign of a lasting friendship. When enmity exists between two men, they never exchange sops or eat at the same table.

Judas, one of Jesus' apostles, dipped his hand in his Master's dish to prove that he was not a traitor. But, according to the gospel story, Jesus knew that he was going to betray him, so he passed a sop to him so that he could point him out.[4]

The best and most delicious dishes were placed before Joseph. He was the governor and the host. Before him were special dishes and trays of food that his semi-nomadic brothers had never seen.

Joseph gave larger portions to his brother Benjamin, simply

---

[4]Mt. 26:23; Jn. 13:26.

because he loved him more than his other brothers. After all, they both came from the same mother. Joseph could no longer restrain his affection toward his brother and began to show partiality and preference for him.

CHAPTER 44

Divining Cup

And put my cup, the silver cup, in the sack's mouth of the youngest, and his corn money. And he did according to the word that Joseph had spoken. As soon as the morning was light, the men were sent away, they and their asses. And when they were gone out of the city, and not yet far off, Joseph said unto his steward, Up, follow after the men; and when thou dost overtake them say unto them, Wherefore have ye rewarded evil for good? Is not this it in which my lord drinketh, and whereby indeed he divineth? Ye have done evil in so doing. Gen. 44:2-5.

In the Near East, kings, princes, and noblemen have individual silver or golden cups for drinking water. Neither the servants nor even other members of the family are allowed to use these cups.

Some of these cups are handed down from one generation to another and, therefore, they are considered not only as heirlooms but also as sacred. Some of these vessels were previously used by famous kings, high priests, and holy men. This custom of special drinking cups for kings and princes prevailed in the Near East until recently.

Soothsayers and men and women with special psychic gifts used these cups for divination and fortune telling. (In the Bible these men and women are referred to as people with familiar spirits.) The cup is filled with water and placed before the inquirer. The medium then gives an oracle that he or she claims comes out of the cup. At times, a small voice may come out of the cup, revealing hidden matters to the inquirer.

The custom of divining by means of the cup is still practiced in the Near East, and many people believe in it. This practice is similar to the use of a crystal ball.

Joseph instructed his servants to put the cup in Benjamin's sack along with the money for the purchase of the wheat (not corn). The King James version translates it as "corn money."

CHAPTER 46

El–God

And he said, I am God, the God of thy father: fear not to go down into Egypt; for I will there make of thee a great nation. Gen. 46:3.

The Eastern Aramaic text reads: "Then he said to him, I am *El,* the God of your father; fear not to go down to Egypt; for I will there make of you a great people."[1] God spoke to Israel (Jacob) in a vision of the night and said to him, "I am El, the God of your father," which meant that it was the God of Isaac.

In patriarchal days, *El* was the name of the God of Israel. The Aramaic noun begins with the letter *aleph*–A. The second letter is *ae,* also an A, and the last consonant is an L. These letters *aleph* and *ae* are interchangeable in the vernacular. *El* might have been derived from *Al,* "upon," which is the root of the adverb *elaiah,* "high." Ancient peoples pictured God as dwelling in high places and riding upon the clouds.[2] ". . . makest the clouds his chariot."[3]

Such was the concept of the ancients about God and his holy attributes when they named him *El* or *Al,* "the Highest," the One who sees the whole universe beneath him.

When Jacob saw the vision of the ladder and the angels, he called the name of the place *Beth-el,* "the house of God."[4] And Jacob's name was changed to Israel, "prince of God."[5]

The Arabic term for God is *Allah;* the Aramaic, *Alaha;* the Assyrian, *Elu.* All the gods of the Gentiles were images and idols that were made of silver, gold, stone, and wood. They were all stationary

---

[1]Gen. 46:3, Eastern Aramaic Peshitta text, Lamsa translation.
[2]See Ex. 24:16, Lev. 16:2.
[3]Ps. 104:3, K. J. V.
[4]Gen. 28:19.
[5]Gen. 32:28.

on the ground. *El* was the high and living God, whose abode was in heaven above all creation, and who was not made by the hands of men.

Closing of the Eyes

I will go down with thee into Egypt; and I will also surely bring thee up again: and Joseph shall put his hand upon thine eyes. Gen. 46:4.

"And Joseph shall put his hand upon thine eyes" is an Aramaic idiom that is still in common use. It means: "He shall close your eyes when you die;" that is, "he shall bury you." When Jacob died, Joseph made the preparations for his burial in the land of Canaan and buried him with his father, Isaac.[6]

One of the highest desires of a Near Eastern father is to have one of his beloved children close his eyes, mourn over him, and bury him. That is why one of Jesus' followers said to him "Lord, suffer me first to go and bury my father."[7] This man's father was not dead. What he was saying was that he wanted to take care of his father at home as long as his father lived and then bury him after his death.[8]

Sixty-Six Souls

All the souls that came with Jacob into Egypt, which came out of his loins, besides Jacob's sons' wives, all the souls were threescore and six; And the sons of Joseph, which were born him in Egypt were two souls: all the souls of the house of Jacob, which came into Egypt, were threescore and ten. Gen. 46:26-27.

---

[6]Gen. 50:1-7.

[7]Mt. 8:21-22, K. J. V.

[8] See Errico and Lamsa, *Aramaic Light on the Gospel of Matthew,* "Burying One's Father," pp. 129-130.

It is interesting to know that there are sixty-six books in the Bible, equivalent to the number of persons who came from Jacob's loins and went down with him into Egypt. The persons, including the children of Joseph, were seventy in all.

The number of the elders of Israel was seventy.[9] Jesus of Nazareth also sent out seventy of his disciples to preach the gospel of God's kingdom.[10] The years of the captivity as foretold by Jeremiah were seventy.[11] There were seventy *shawoay* (weeks) in Daniel's prophecy.[12] The number seventy must have been a sacred and fortunate number in those days.

Pastoral People

That ye shall say, Thy servants' trade hath been about cattle from our youth even until now, both we, and also our fathers: that ye may dwell in the land of Goshen; for every shepherd is an abomination unto the Egyptians. Gen. 46:34.

The Hebrews who went down to dwell in Egypt, like their ancestors, were a pastoral people. They knew no other occupation than raising sheep and cattle.

On the other hand, pastoral life or sheep-raising was an abomination to the Egyptians, who lived in the fertile lands and whose occupation was agriculture. This is still true of the mountain and plains people in Palestine and other lands in the Near East. The city people seldom drank sheep milk; they preferred cows' milk.

Joseph knew that the Egyptians were not interested in the lush pasture lands of Goshen that belonged to the crown. City people usually were engaged in arts, crafts, farming, and manufacture of

---

[9]Ex. 18:25, Num. 11:16.
[10]Lk. 10:1.
[11]Jer. 25:11.
[12]Dan. 9:24.

household articles that they exchanged for butter, wool, cheese, and other products.[13] They looked down on nomad people, their occupation, and their way of life.

---

[13]Gen. 47:3.

CHAPTER 47

Slavery

Wherefore shall we die before thine eyes, both we and our land? Buy us and our land for bread, and we and our land will be servants unto Pharaoh: and give us seed, that we may live, and not die, that the land be not desolate. Gen. 47:19.

In biblical days, when families found that all their substance was gone and there was no hope of borrowing money or wheat, they sold themselves and their children and thus became the slaves of the lenders. Both men and women were traded for money, wheat, and other commodities. Joseph was sold by his brothers for twenty pieces of silver.[1]

Slavery prevailed in many Near and Middle Eastern lands as well as African lands until recent years. Men and women were sold and bought in the markets, and debtors sold themselves to their creditors.

The Mosaic law sanctioned the sale of poverty-stricken Hebrews, but enjoined the purchasers to treat them well.[2]

---

[1]Gen. 37:28, 45:4.
[2]Lev. 25:39-43, Isa. 52:3.

195

CHAPTER 48

Laying on of Hands

And Israel stretched out his right hand, and laid it upon Ephraim's head, who was the younger, and his left hand upon Manasseh's head, guiding his hands wittingly; for Manasseh was the firstborn. Gen. 48:14.

Laying on of hands in Semitic languages has several meanings:

(1) To transmit God's blessings from one person to another. The physical contact helps the person to receive the blessing. The hand symbolizes power and authority.

(2) To arrest. "And laid their hands on the apostles, and put them in the common prison."[1] In this case, it means they seized them. "When they sought to lay hands on him" means, "to arrest him."[2]

(3) To appoint or ordain.[3] In most cases in the New Testament, it is used as a symbol of blessing and healing.[4]

(4) To single out a guilty person; hence, to accuse.

Jacob Delivered from Evil

The Angel which redeemed me from all evil, bless the lads; and let my name be named on them, and the name of my fathers Abraham and Isaac; and let them grow into a multitude in the midst of the earth. Gen. 48:16.

The reference is to the evil that Jacob had done to his brother, Esau, and to his father, Isaac, when he deceived them about the birthright.[5]

---

[1]Acts 5:18, K. J. V.
[2]Mt. 21:46, K. J. V.
[3]Acts 13:1-3.
[4]Mt. 19:13, Lk. 4:40.
[5]Gen. 27:12-27.

Jacob had also taken justice into his own hands and had acquired some of Laban's cattle and sheep by some device unknown to Laban and the people of Haran.

Jacob acknowledged his faults and sins and sought God's forgiveness. God forgave him and blessed him and granted him power to bless others. The angel of the Lord blessed him and called his name Israel, "prince of God," and delivered him from all his enemies. So, Jacob prays that the messenger of God that had delivered him from all evils would also bless and deliver his grandsons.

Blessing with the Right Hand

And when Joseph saw that his father laid his right hand upon the head of Ephraim, it displeased him: and he held up his father's hand, to remove it from Ephraim's head unto Manassesh's head. Gen. 48:17.

Among Semitic peoples the right hand is symbolic of blessing and right action, and the left hand is a bad omen. The queen sits on the right hand of the king, and honored guests sit on the right hand of the host. The right hand also symbolizes power. ". . . with the pleasure of victory of thy right hand."[6] "If I forget you, O Jerusalem let my right hand forget me."[7]

All blessings are bestowed upon people by placing of the right hand on them. Joseph was alarmed when he saw that his father had placed his right hand upon the head of his younger son, so he tried to remove it and place it on the head of his elder son, Manasseh; but Jacob knew what he was doing. Being a seer, he saw that Ephraim would be greater than Manasseh, Joseph's firstborn.

---

[6]Ps. 16:11, Eastern Aramaic Peshitta text, Lamsa translation.
[7]Ps. 137:5, Eastern Aramaic Peshitta text, Lamsa translation.

CHAPTER 49

Patriarchs–Prophets

And Jacob called unto his sons, and said, Gather yourselves together, that I may tell you that which shall befall you in the last days. Gen. 49:1.

All the Hebrew patriarchs were prophets. They saw visions, interpreted dreams, foretold things to come, warned the people of impending disaster, and admonished them to walk in the way of God. They were divinely guided and, during times of famine and disaster, were led to safety.

The Lord God had revealed the divine plans for the salvation of humankind to Abraham, Isaac, and Jacob. He had assured them that by their seed all the nations of the world would be blessed. He also revealed to them what was to take place after them.

Jacob not only could foretell future events, but he also knew how to interpret dreams for them. It was he who taught Joseph how to interpret dreams and reveal hidden matters.

The Hebrew patriarchs lived a simple life, and they lived in a very close relationship with God. They believed in God and walked in the way that the divine presence revealed to them. God communed with them because they were open to receive and follow through with all the guidance they received. God revealed to them matters that were hidden from the eyes of other peoples and races who were far stronger and more advanced.

Sceptre

The sceptre shall not depart from Judah, nor a lawgiver from between his feet, until Shiloh come, and unto him shall the gathering of the people be. Gen. 49:10.

The sceptre is the symbol of authority or leadership. Judah was the most brilliant among his eleven brothers. He was a gifted speaker and a statesman. When Joseph wanted to detain Benjamin, Judah stood before Joseph and made an excellent appeal on behalf of his brother that so moved the heart of the governor general, he could no longer restrain his tears.[1]

Judah was second only to Joseph in wisdom and understanding. Reuben had committed adultery with one of his father's concubines and by so doing was challenging his father's authority; therefore, Jacob had discarded him as an heir. The tribe of Judah was to be the most important of the twelve tribes. Kings and lawgivers were to come forth out of Judah's descendants until the coming of the promised one. The Aramaic text reads: "Until the coming of the One to whom the sceptre belongs, to whom the Gentiles shall look forward." The word *Shiloh* is not in the Eastern Aramaic Peshitta text.

Jacob, as a patriarch and a seer, saw the fulfillment of Israel's mission. His descendants were to rule until the coming of the great King, the Messiah, who was to establish a universal kingdom and become a light to the Gentiles and to the world in general.[2]

The term *Shiloh* might be derived from *shaal,* "to ask." Shealia, *Shiloh,* means "that which the people had prayed for," "a deliverer;" that is, "Messiah." Shiloh was a city in Ephraim where the Israelites assembled and erected the tabernacle.[3]

In the Near East, when people visit a shrine they present offerings, make wishes, and ask God to grant them the desires of their hearts, as in the case of Hannah described in 1 Samuel 1:10-11.

LAWGIVER BETWEEN HIS FEET

The Aramaic and Hebrew term for "law" also means "light."

---

[1]Gen. 44:16-34.
[2]Isa. 9:1-2.
[3]Jos. 18:1, 19:51.

199

"Thy word is a lamp to my feet and a light to my path."[4]

Until the late 1920s, the streets in the Near East were not repaired or cleaned. Rubbish and stones were thrown into the streets. Only when kings or princes entered a city were the inhabitants directed to clean the streets. Therefore, when people walked with the king, they carried a lamp with them, bending down and holding it between their feet so that they may not stumble. The streets of the ancient cities were generally narrow and crooked. People could hardly walk on them without a candle or a lamp. In many Eastern countries, one could see a servant walking ahead of his master, bending down and holding the lamp so that his master would not stumble.

The Lord God always provided a lawgiver for Israel—the descendants of David. Without the law Israel would not have been able to execute justice. There were two copies of the book of the Torah, one for the priest and the other for the king.

According to Scripture, the Torah is the light of God that enables humanity to see justice, peace, and equity for all. When people walk in the light they never stumble. Jesus' teachings were a continuation and further explanations of the Torah that brought hope and a greater clarity to his people. His way of life and conduct were a light to men and women who gathered around him.

Red with Wine and White with Milk

Binding his foal unto the vine, and his ass's colt unto the choice vine; he washed his garments in wine, and his clothes in the blood of grapes; His eyes shall be red with wine, and his teeth white with milk. Gen. 49:11-12.

These verses should not be taken literally. The author of Genesis used colloquial expressions. "He washed his garments in wine" and "his eyes shall be red with wine" are figures of speech, meaning that he will inhabit a land graced with many vineyards and that he will

---

[4]Ps. 119:105, K. J. V.

200

have plenty of wine to drink.

Semites often say, "He swims in oil," which means, "He has plenty of butter or olive oil." "He bathes in milk" means, "He has an abundance of milk."

In the Near East, those who have vineyards use considerable wine at the table. In the ancient days, wine was used because of the lack of water. Our English term about an individual who is "red eyed" has a negative meaning and refers to someone who has imbibed too much wine.

The land of Judah was noted for good vineyards. The Hebron region was the place from which the Hebrew spies brought grapes to Moses and the elders of Israel.[5]

"His teeth white with milk" is a Near Eastern idiom which means, "He shall have an abundance of flocks and plenty of milk."

In biblical days, the economy was based on sheep, milk, wool, and other by products. Also, the main diet of the people consisted of milk, buttermilk, cream, cheese, and butter, and they possessed teeth that were pearly white and in good condition.

A Mighty Man

Issachar is a strong ass couching down between two burdens.
Gen. 49:14.

The Aramaic text reads: "Issachar is a mighty man couching by the highways."[6] *Gabbarah* means, "a mighty man." The Aramaic word for "ass" is *hamarah*. The letters *heth* and *gamel* resemble one another when placed before a word. The error was created by the close similarity of the two Aramaic words. When a manuscript is too old or mutilated, as they often are, letters and words are confused with one another. The scribes and the translators had some difficulty

---

[5]Num. 13:23.
[6]Gen. 49:14, Eastern Aramaic Peshitta text, Lamsa translation.

in ascertaining the meaning of some of the words.

In the Near East, it would be repulsive to call a person an ass. At the same time, no father at his deathbed would call his son a donkey, especially when he is blessing him before he departs this life.

Dan–a Judge

Dan shall judge his people, as one of the tribes of Israel. Dan shall be a serpent by the way, an adder on the path, that biteth the horse heels, so that his rider shall fall backward. Gen. 49:16-17.

Dan in Aramaic means "to judge." *Dyana* means "a judge." Rachael had named the son of Bilhah, her handmaid, "Dan." She felt the Lord had judged between her and her sister, Leah.[7]

Dan would become a judge, not only over his own tribe, but over all the tribes of Israel. Samson was of the tribe of Dan and became a judge over all Israel.[8]

The Danites, however, were an impulsive and intemperate tribe. They were like a serpent by the road and like an adder on the path. They were dangerous and unprincipled. When a snake bites a horse, the animal rears and the rider is thrown from his horse. Therefore, the Danite tribe is compared to the snake and adder.

For example, a biblical episode clearly depicts the nature and characteristics of this tribe. The Danites were given only a small portion of the land of Canaan after the conquest; years later, the clan moved northward and encountered a people on the border of Lebanon, a people of peace. These people had no fortifications because they did no evil and did not expect evil to befall them. But when the Danites saw that these tribal people were unarmed and harmless, they slew all of them and possessed their land.[9]

---

[7]Gen. 30:5-6.
[8]Judges 13:2-24.
[9]Judges 18:7-29.

Joseph, a Cultured Man

Joseph is a fruitful bough, even a fruitful bough by a well; whose branches run over the wall. Gen. 49:22.

The Aramaic text reads, "Joseph is a disciplined son, an educated son" [or "a cultured man"], meaning that Joseph had been well-tutored to become the chief of the tribe and a successor to his father, Jacob. This is the reason Joseph wore a coat of long sleeves embroidered with colors. This appointment bestowed on Joseph by Jacob created a great deal of envy and jealously among his brothers, so much so that they despised him.

Jacob had taught Joseph to interpret visions and dreams and to know how to behave in the presence of princes and rulers. As a lad, he had received God's revelations. Joseph was called by God to a great mission to save his people during a severe famine.[10]

Isaac was taught by his father, Abraham, who was a learned man and a prophet of God. According to Near Eastern extra biblical writings, Abraham had belonged to a well educated Babylonian priestly family.

Joseph's education and his good manners helped him rise to the very high position in the land of Egypt.

Stretched out His Feet

And when Jacob had made an end of commanding his sons, he gathered up his feet into the bed, and yielded up the ghost, and was gathered unto his people. Gen. 49:33.

The Eastern Aramaic text reads: "He stretched his feet on his bed." This is a Semitic idiom which means, "he died." In the Near East when a sick man is near death, they stretch out his feet before he

---

[10]Gen. 50:20.

203

passes away.

Jacob had been sick in bed for some time when he summoned his sons to his bedside. When Joseph and his other sons came to see him, he sat up on the bed.

CHAPTER 50

Egyptian Mourning

And when the inhabitants of the land, the Canaanites, saw the mourning in the floor of Atad, they said, This is a grievous mourning to the Egyptians: wherefore the name of it was called Abelmizraim, which is beyond Jordan. Gen. 50:11.

Abel-mizraim means, "the mourning of the Egyptians." *Abilotha* means, "mourning, lamentation, to wail for the dead." Near Easterners mourn for many days and raise their voices in wailing over the departed. Canaan, at this time, must have been a protectorate under Egypt.

Under God

And Joseph said unto them, Fear not: for am I in the place of God? Gen. 50:19.

The Eastern Aramaic text reads: "But Joseph said to them, Fear not; for I am a servant of God. But as for you, you thought evil against me; but God meant it for good to do as he has done this day, to save many lives."[1]

Joseph did not say to his brother, "For am I in the place of God?" What Joseph meant is that he also was a human being under the care and guidance of God. His brothers were so frightened that they prostrated themselves before him as one would do when worshiping God.

Joseph saw that his vision of the sheaves and the stars and the moon were fulfilled, but he refused to see his brothers paying

---

[1]Gen. 50:19-20, Eastern Aramaic Peshitta text, Lamsa translation.

obeisance to him, for he was, after all, a human being like each of them and a servant of God. Joseph was a loving and generously kind man, who understood the ways of God and divine inner guidance.

BIBLIOGRAPHY

Alter, Michael J. *What is the Purpose of Creation? A Jewish Anthology*. Northvale, New Jersey: Jason Aronson Inc., 1991.

Aviezer, Nathan. *In the Beginning: Biblical Creation and Science*. Hoboken, New Jersey: KATV Publishing House, Inc., 1990.

Batto, Bernard F. *Slaying the Dragon: Mythmaking in the Biblical Tradition*. Louisville, Kentucky: Westminster/John Knox Press, 1992.

Berlin, Adele. *The Dynamics of Biblical Parallelism*. Bloomington, Indiana: Indiana University Press, 1985.

Blenkinsopp, Joseph. *The Pentateuch: An Introduction to the First Books of the Bible*. New York: Doubleday, 1992.

Carus, Paul. *The History of the Devil and the Idea of the Devil*. LaSalle, Illinois: Open Court Publishing Co., 1900.

Cassuto, Umberto. *A Commentary on the Book of Genesis, Part One: From Adam to Noah*. Translated by Israel Abrahams. Jerusalem: Magnes Press, 1989.
_____ *The Documentary Hypothesis: Eight Lectures*. Translated by Israel Abrahams. Jerusalem: Magnes Press, 1983.

Davies, Paul. *God and the New Physics*. New York: Simon & Schuster, 1983.
_____ *The Mind of God: The Scientific Basis for a Rational World*. New York: Simon & Schuster, 1992.

Errico, Rocco A. *The Message of Matthew: An Annotated Parallel Aramaic-English Gospel of Matthew*. Smyrna, Georgia (formerly,

Santa Fe, New Mexico): Noohra Foundation, 1991.

Forrester-Brown, James S. *The Two Creation Stories in Genesis: A Study of their Symbolism.* Berkeley, California: Shambhala, 1974.

Fox, Everett. *In the Beginning: A New English Rendition of the Book of Genesis.* New York: Schocken Books, 1983.

Freedman, David Noel, Editor-in-Chief. *Anchor Bible Dictionary.* New York: Doubleday, 1992.
_____ *The Unity of the Hebrew Bible.* Ann Arbor, Michigan: University of Michigan Press, 1991.

Frymer-Kensky, Tikva. *In the Wake of the Goddesses: Women, Culture and the Biblical Transformation of Pagan Myth.* New York: The Free Press, 1992.

Graves, Robert and Raphael Patai. *Hebrew Myths: The Book of Genesis.* New York: McGraw-Hill Books, 1966.

Heisenberg, Werner. *Physics and Beyond.* New York: Harper & Row, 1971.
_____ *Physics & Philosophy: The Revolution in Modern Science.* New York: Harper & Row, 1962.

Heschel, Abraham Joshua. *Man is Not Alone: A Philosophy of Religion.* New York: Noonday Press, 1990.

Holmes, Ernest S. *Your Invisible Power.* Los Angeles, California: Science of Mind Publications, 1974.

Keightley, Alan. *Into Every Life a Little Zen Must Fall: A Christian Looks to Alan Watts and the East.* London: Wisdom Publications, 1986.

Knight, Douglas A. and Gene M. Tucker, Editors. *The Hebrew Bible and Its Modern Interpreters*. Chico, California: Scholars Press, 1985.

Laqueur, Thomas. *Making Sex: Body and Gender from the Greeks to Freud*. Cambridge, Massachusetts: Harvard University. Press, 1990.

Larue, Gerald A. *Ancient Myth and Modern Life*. Long Beach, California: Centerline Press, 1988.

Levenson, Jon D. *Creation and the Persistence of Evil: The Jewish Drama of Divine Omnipotence*. San Francisco, California: Harper & Row, 1988.
_____ *Sinai and Zion: An Entry into the Jewish Bible*. San Francisco, California: Harper & Row, 1985.

Halpern, Baruch and John D. Levenson, Editors. *Traditions in Transformation: Turning Points in Biblical Faith*. Winona Lake, Indiana: Eisenbrauns, 1981.

Hitti, Philip K. *The Near East in History: A 5000 Year Story*. Princeton, New Jersey: D. Van Nostrand Co., 1961.

Lamsa, George M. *Old Testament Light: A Scriptural Commentary Based on the Aramaic of the Ancient Peshitta Text*. Englewood Cliffs, New Jersey: Prentice-Hall, 1964.

Mendel, Arthur P. *Vision and Violence*. Ann Arbor, Michigan: University of Michigan Press, 1992.

Mettinger, Tryggve, N.D. *In Search of God: The Meaning and Message of the Everlasting Names*. Translated by Frederick H. Cryer. Philadelphia, Pennsylvania: Fortress Press, 1988.

Niditch, Susan. *Chaos to Cosmos: Studies in Biblical Patterns of Creation*. Chico, California: Scholars Press, 1985.

O'Brien, Joan and Wilfred Major. *In The Beginning: Creation Myths from Ancient Mesopotamia, Israel and Greece*. Chico, California: Scholars Press, 1982.

O'Connor, M. P. *Hebrew Verse Structure*. Winona Lake, Indiana: Eisenbrauns, 1980.

Oden, Robert A., Jr. *The Bible without Theology: The Theological Tradition and Alternatives to It*. San Francisco, California: Harper & Row, 1987.

Plaut, W. Gunther. *The Torah: Genesis, A Modern Commentary*. New York: Jewish Publication Society, 1974.

Pritchard, James B. *Ancient Near Eastern Texts: Relating to the Old Testament,* 2nd Edition with supplement. Princeton, New Jersey: University Press, 1978.

Radday, Yehuda and Haim Shore. *Genesis: An Authorship Study*. Rome: Biblical Institute Press, 1985.

Rihbany, A. M. *The Syrian Christ*. Boston, Massachusetts: Houghton-Mifflin Co., 1916.

Sarna, Nahum M. *Genesis: The JPS Torah Commentary*. New York: Jewish Publication Society, 1989.

Smith, Mark S. *The Early History of God: Yahweh and the Other Deities in Ancient Israel*. New York: Harper-Collins, 1990.

Speiser, E. A. *Genesis: A New Translation with Introduction and Commentary*. Garden City, New York: Doubleday, 1964.

Sternberg, Meir. *The Poetics of Biblical Narrative: Ideological Literature and the Drama of Reading*. Bloomington, Indiana: Indiana

University Press, 1985.

Trible, Phyllis. *God and the Rhetoric of Sexuality*. Philadelphia, Pennsylvia: Fortress Press, 1978.

Von Franz, Marie-Louise. *Creation Myths: Patterns of Creativity*. Dallas, Texas: Spring Publications 1986.

Weber, Max. *The Religion of China*. Translated and edited by Hans H. Gerth. Glenco, Illinois: Free Press, 1951.

Westermann, Claus. *Genesis 1–11: A Commentary*. Translated by John J. Schullion, S. J. Minneapolis, Minnesota: Augsburg Publishing House, 1990.
_____ *Genesis: An introduction*. Translated by John J. Schullion, S.J. Minneapolis, Minnesota: Fortress Press, 1992.

Westman, Heinz. *The Structure of Biblical Myths: The Onto-genesis of the Psyche*. Dallas, Texas: Spring Publications, 1983.

Williams, James G. *The Bible, Violence and the Sacred: Liberation from the Myth of Sanctioned Violence*. San Francisco, California: Harper & Row, 1991.

Wolf, Fred Alan. *Taking the Quantum Leap: The New Physics for Nonscientists*. San Francisco, California: Harper & Row, 1981.

Zeitlan, Irving M. *Ancient Judaism*. Oxford: Polity Press, Basil Blackwell, 1984.

ABOUT THE AUTHOR
George M. Lamsa

George M. Lamsa, Th.D., a renowned native Assyrian scholar of the Holy Bible, translator, lecturer, ethnologist, and author, was born August 5, 1892 in a civilization with customs, manners and language almost identical to those in the time of Jesus. His native tongue, Aramaic, was filled with similar idioms and parables, untouched by the outside world in 1900 years.

Until World War 1, his people living in that part of the ancient biblical lands that today is known as Kurdistan, in the basin of the rivers Tigris and Euphrates, retained the simple nomadic life as in the days of the Hebrew patriarchs. Only at the beginning of the 20th century did the isolated segment of the once great Assyrian Empire learn of the discovery of America and the Reformation in Germany.

Likewise, until that same time, this ancient culture of early Christians was unknown to the Western world, and the Aramaic language was thought to be dead. But in this so-called "Cradle of Civilization," primitive biblical customs and Semitic culture, cut off from the world, were preserved.

Lamsa's primary upbringing as a boy was to tend the lambs. But as the first-born in his family, while yet an infant he was dedicated to God by his devout mother. Years after her death, when Lamsa was 12 years of age, her vow was renewed by native tribesmen, an ox killed, and its blood rubbed on his forehead. Lamsa claimed this vow to God had always been part of him. "God's hand," he affirmed, "has been steadfastly on my shoulder, guiding me in the divine work."

Lamsa's formal education and studies began under the priests and deacons of the ancient Church of the East. Later he graduated with the highest honors ever bestowed from the Archbishop of Canterbury's Colleges in Iran and in Turkey, with the degree of Bachelor of Arts. Lamsa never married, but dedicated his life to "God's calling." He spoke eight languages and his lowest grade in any subject was 99.

At the beginning of World War 1, when Turkey began its invasions, Lamsa was forced to flee the Imperial University at Constantinople where he was studying. He went to South America where he endured great hardships during those years. He knew but three words in Spanish at that time—water, work, and bread. As best as he could he existed—in the British Merchant Marine for a time, then working on railroads, in mines, and later in printing shops, a trade he had learned while attending college in Iran.

After arriving in the United States in his early 20s, Lamsa worked by day as a printer, and by night he went to school. He later studied at the Episcopal Theological Seminary in Alexandria, Virginia, and at Dropsie College in Philadelphia.

It was through his struggles, during these years, with the English idioms that Lamsa gradually launched into his "life's work" of translating the Holy Bible from Aramaic into English. Yet many years were to pass before the world received his translations.

First as a lecturer in churches and seminaries, in halls and auditoriums, before statesmen, theologians, groups of artists, actors and others, Lamsa received recognition as a poet-philosopher and as an authority on all phases of Near Eastern civilization.

It was his own inner compulsion, and the urging of hundreds who heard him, that drove him forward and brought about—after 30 years of labor, research and study—his translation of the Holy Bible from a branch of the ancient Aramaic language that Jesus and the earliest Christians used.

There were times, when the idioms in the manuscripts could not be given correct English equivalents, that he was temporarily stopped in his translations. It was Lamsa's firm belief that his translation from Aramaic would bring people closer to the Word of God and would facilitate understanding between the East and the West. For forty years, he produced commentaries and many other works based on the Aramaic language. The last ten years of his life, Dr. Lamsa tutored and prepared Dr. Rocco A. Errico to continue with the Aramaic approach to Scripture. He left this earthly life on September 22, 1975, in Turlock, California.

ABOUT THE AUTHOR
Rocco A. Errico

Dr. Rocco A. Errico is an ordained minister, international lecturer and author, spiritual counselor, and one of the nation's leading Biblical scholars working from the original Aramaic *Peshitta* texts. For ten years he studied intensively with Dr. George M. Lamsa, Th.D., (1890-1975), world-renowned Assyrian biblical scholar and translator of the *Holy Bible from the Ancient Eastern Text*. Dr. Errico is proficient in Aramaic and Hebrew exegesis, helping thousands of readers and seminar participants understand how the Semitic context of culture, language, idioms, symbolism, mystical style, psychology, and literary amplification—the *Seven Keys* that unlock the Bible—are essential to understanding this ancient spiritual document.

Dr. Errico is the recipient of numerous awards and academic degrees, including a Doctorate in Philosophy from the School of Christianity in Los Angeles; a Doctorate in Divinity from St. Ephrem's Institute in Sweden; and a Doctorate in Sacred Theology from the School of Christianity in Los Angeles. In 1993, the American Apostolic University College of Seminarians awarded him a Doctorate of Letters. He also holds a special title of Teacher, Prime Exegete, *Maplana d'miltha dalaha*, among the Federation of St. Thomas Christians of the order of Antioch. In 2002, Dr. Errico was inducted into the Morehouse College Collegium of Scholars.

Dr. Errico is a featured speaker at conferences, symposia, and seminars throughout the United States, Canada, Mexico and Europe and has been a regular contributor for over 25 years to *Science of Mind Magazine*, a monthly journal founded in 1927. He began his practice as an ordained minister and pastoral counselor in the mid-1950s and during the next three decades served in churches and missions in Missouri, Texas, Mexico, and California. Throughout his public work, Dr. Errico has stressed the nonsectarian, *open* interpretation of Biblical spirituality, prying it free from 2000 years of rigid orthodoxy, which, according to his research, is founded on incorrect translations of the original Aramaic texts.

In 1970, Dr. Errico established the Noohra Foundation in San Antonio, Texas, as a non-profit, non-sectarian spiritual-educational organization devoted to helping people of all faiths to understand the Near Eastern background and Aramaic interpretation of the Bible. In 1976, Dr. Errico relocated the Noohra Foundation in Irvine, California, where it flourished for the next 17 years. For seven years, the Noohra Foundation operated in Santa Fe, New Mexico, and in September 2001, it relocated to Smyrna, Georgia, where Dr. Errico is Dean of Biblical Studies for Dr. Barbara King's School of Ministry—Hillside Chapel and Truth Center in Atlanta.

Under the auspices of the Noohra Foundation, Dr. Errico continues to lecture for colleges, civic groups and churches of various denominations in the United States, Canada, Mexico and Europe.

———————

For a complimentary catalog of Aramaic Bible translations, books, audio and video cassettes, CDs and DVDs, to receive mailings of classes, retreats and future publications, or for any other inquiries, write, call, or email the Noohra Foundation. Those interested in scheduling Dr. Errico for a personal appearance may also contact:

Noohra Foundation
PMB 343
4480 South Cobb Dr SE Ste H
Smyrna, Georgia 30080

Phone: 678-945-4006
Fax: 678-945-4966

email: inf   ahoo.com
Noc   com

NOOHRA FOUNDATION
4480 S Cobb Dr Ste H #343
Smyrna GA 30080 - www.noohra.org
Ph: 1-888-992-8161, 678-945-4006
noohrafoundation@mail.com

In addition to this commentary, the Noohra Foundation is pleased to offer the following books by Dr. Rocco A. Errico and Dr. George M. Lamsa.

NEW TESTAMENT COMMENTARIES BY DR. ERRICO & DR. LAMSA

(1) **Aramaic Light on the Gospel of Matthew** (2) **Aramaic Light on the Gospels of Mark and Luke** (3) **Aramaic Light on the Gospel of John** (4) **Aramaic Light on the Acts of the Apostles,** (5) **Aramaic Light on Romans through 2 Corinthians** (6) **Aramaic Light on Galatians through Hebrews** (7) **Aramaic Light on James through Revelation**.

BOOKS BY DR. ERRICO:

LET THERE BE LIGHT: The Seven Keys

In this illuminating work, Dr. Errico presents seven key insights to understand the allusions, parables, and teachings of the Bible, opening the door to the ancient Aramaic world from which the Bible emerged.

AND THERE WAS LIGHT

Like its predecessor, *Let There Be Light*, this book unlocks puzzling passages with the Seven Keys. The Bible now becomes clearer and more relevant for Western readers, and the teaching ministry and parables of Jesus come alive as never before.

SETTING A TRAP FOR GOD: The Aramaic Prayer of Jesus

Dr. Errico explains the meaning of the Lord's Prayer based on the Aramaic language and ancient culture of the Near East. Discover the way of peace, health, and prosperity as you learn to "set a trap" for the inexhaustible power of God.

THE MYSTERIES OF CREATION: The Genesis Story

A challenging new look at the processes and mysteries of the primal creation account. Dr. Errico uses his own direct translation from the Aramaic-Peshitta text of Genesis 1:1-31 and 2:1-3.

THE MESSAGE OF MATTHEW: An Annotated Parallel Aramaic-English Gospel of Matthew

Dr. Errico's translation of the ancient Aramaic Peshitta text of Matthew with illuminating annotations. The English translation is on the left side of the page with footnotes. The Aramaic text is on the right.

CLASSICAL ARAMAIC: Book I

Learn to read and write the language of Jesus in a self-teachable format.

Classical Aramaic is a practical grammar that prepares you to read the New Testament in Jesus' own native tongue.

LA ANTIGUA ORACIÓN ARAMEA DE JESÚS: El Padrenuestro

Dr. Errico's own translation into Spanish of his book *The Ancient Aramaic Prayer of Jesus.*

DAS ARAMAISCHE VATERUNSER

German translation and publication of *Setting a Trap for God.*

ES WERDE LICHT

German translation and publication of *Let There Be Light.*

OTTO ACCORDI CON DIO: il Padre Nostro originario

Italian translation and publication of *Setting a Trap for God.*

BOOKS BY DR. LAMSA

THE HOLY BIBLE FROM THE ANCIENT EASTERN TEXT

The entire Bible translated directly into English from Aramaic, the language of Jesus. There are approximately 12,000 major differences between this English translation and the many traditional versions of the Bible.

IDIOMS IN THE BIBLE EXPLAINED and A KEY TO THE ORIGINAL GOSPELS

Two books in one. In Book 1 (*Idioms in the Bible Explained*) Dr. Lamsa explains nearly 1000 crucial idioms and colloquialisms of Eastern speech that will enrich reading of the Bible for student and general reader alike.

Book 2 (*A Key to the Original Gospels*) explains how the gospels were written, the reason for two different genealogies, the conflicting stories of the birth of Jesus, and more.

THE SHEPHERD OF ALL: The Twenty-Third Psalm

Based on his own personal experience as a shepherd, Dr. Lamsa interprets what many consider the most beautiful, moving and meaningful psalm in the light of Eastern biblical customs.

NEW TESTAMENT ORIGIN

Dr. Lamsa presents his theory for Aramaic as the original written language of the New Testament.